DISPLAYED SPACES

DISPLAYED SPACES

NEW MEANS OF ARCHITECTURE
PRESENTATION THROUGH EXHIBITIONS

edited by Roberto Gigliotti

FOREWORD

A city at a crossroads – More than a thousand years after its foundation, the city of Bolzano – a city of about 100,000 inhabitants situated half way between Austria and Italy as significant pole (and capital) of an Italian region with political autonomy – stands, embarrassed, in front of a crossroads representative of an important decision that will have relevant repercussions on its development and future. By virtue of a new, never applied before, regional zoning law, a strategical and central area in the proximity of the railway and bus stations has been made available for an intervention of radical transformation, to be carried out by private investors under the supervision of the public administration[1].
The real estate investment could radically transform the image of the city and is potentially capable of generating an economic effect of remarkable size. Several parties are involved: the Municipality, an international financial company already known for its part in having constructed a large shopping mall in the centre of the twin capital of Innsbruck just across the border, as well as local investors, an international *starchitect* commissioned by the principal investor to give shape and meaning to the space specified in the project, the (public and private) owners of some of the surrounding buildings and – last but not least – the citizens who will *inhabit* the spaces made available for them (or maybe just for some of them?) as a result of this large-scale financial intervention. Hence the first thing that happens is that an alternative network of partners capable of submitting an alternative project to the public administration is established.

1 The Bozen Bolzano Autonomous Province approved the law quoted in the text in July 2013. The entire sequence of events is extensively documented in the local press.

The real estate intervention under consideration that foresees the demolition of certain public buildings and of an old hotel dating back to the fifties, as well as the redevelopment of the old bus station, and the construction of a *megastore,* a new hotel, luxury flats and office spaces, generates straightaway an intense public debate. Contrasting positions in regards to the *virtuosity* of the intervention arise in public opinion, also because of the anticipated elimination of a large surface of the railway station park (integrated into the city structure ever since the arrival of the railway in the middle of the nineteenth century). The effects of constructing a shopping mall of this dimension on the equilibrium of an already wavering trade market and economy should also be considered (although in a territory that from many points of view could be considered privileged, we are, after all, all subjected to experiencing an economic crisis of transnational scale that threatens the stability of small commercial activities in a historical centre already exposed to the effects of gentrification).

An exhibition – Since the first public appearances of the private investor and his initial statements, reams of ink have been written on the sequence of circumstances roughly outlined above. The local press dedicates considerable space to it, while supporters of the project have given life to a public initiative that organises meetings among the interested parties. The principal investor – from his side – starts a series of initiatives directed at convincing public opinion of how good his endeavour is, for example through the production of film clips, inserts in the local newspapers and, obviously, an alluring and in-depth web site.

In addition to the efforts to sway public opinion just mentioned, there is also an exhaustive exhibition on the project – and on everything that it could tangibly become once realized, once, that is, the world of drafting and representation have been left behind.
The exhibition displays in-depth documentation about this future real estate intervention in a prestigious space in the city centre. Study and final models, photorealistic computer generated renderings, explanatory diagrams, technical drawings and the whole apparatus necessary to deliver as much information on the project as possible are arranged – accompanied by seductive background music – throughout the exhibition space in a carefully lit setting where every displayed object plays a skillfully staged part in the scenography of a convincing presentation. It is not necessary to linger here on the inevitable use (abuse, manipulation?) of the instruments of representation in order to reproduce in convincing and captivating images an architectural idea that could only potentially exist in reality. What for me is important to emphasize here – and that serves to justify this preamble that might otherwise seem only marginally pertinent to the topic of this publication, that is the outcome of research on contemporary practices of architecture exhibitions – is precisely the investor's decision to utilise, together with all the other communication mechanisms, also that of the exhibition as a means for violently entering the public sphere.

What is an exhibition? – Literature on the exhibition is vast and exhaustive and I will make no attempt to resume discussion of questions already addressed in previous important writings. Instead I wish to refer to a few relevant issues to the subject of this study. An exhibition – the translation in spatial sequences, by means of a designer, of the thoughts of a curator – is a system of communication that, thanks to its immersive character, makes a physical and personal experience possible to the public that visits it. To exhibit means to communicate within a narrative space in which "the author and the audience share a special relation. The maker brings an environment to life where the visitor then finds himself. He or she enters a space-time constellation of material means that have been packed with narrative potential by the maker. The expressive power of such a spatial arrangement will only unfold when the visitor takes the time to pay attention and starts participating" (Oudsten, 2012). In the exhibition the receptivity of the visitor is augmented and his/her experience of what has been exhibited is built on the reciprocal relationships between the observer, the object observed, and the space containing the event. When we move through an exhibition space we see, interpret and define connections between the things (generally originals) that have been arranged around us. An exhibition is capable of making visible also things that are not found, with us, in the exhibition space.

What is an architecture exhibition? – In recent years, as the diffusion of study courses and conferences on exhibiting and curating confirms, also architecture exhibitions have become the subject of study and observation and we witness the widening of a specialised literature on this subject[2]. Also in architecture exhibitions, starting from the selection gesture, the exhibited objects are transferred to a context which is not the one from which they were generated, and they tell stories that articulate around the relationship between the objects themselves, the visitors and the exhibition space. Furthermore, we cannot ignore that architecture in itself (or, better said, the built environment) cannot, due to its nature, be contained in the exhibition space. As Zardini remarked, it has become rhetorical to state that an architecture exhibition shows things that are not present and are located elsewhere (2012) and that the artefacts exhibited in an architecture exhibition, as Jean Louis Cohen argues in a conversation with Yve-Alain Bois, Denis Hollier and Rosalind Krauss, are "indices of something which, when the work is built, is out there" (Bois, Hollier, Krauss 1999). Nevertheless, from these statements a series of articulated reflections opens up on the meaning of exhibiting architecture, on the numerous possibilities in the field of communication and representation that are linked with this apparent contradiction, and on the issues related to the fact that showing architecture requires a series of mediation procedures and the translation of the exhibited object into artefacts that can be experienced within the space of the show.

Exhibition studies, as well as further reflections on the topic, allow us to identify certain possible forms that the architecture exhibition has assumed over the course of its development and that have led up to the present-day landscape. Such studies and analysis derive from approaches – among others – which, on the

2 Di Carlo T. 2010 (ed.), Levy A. & Menking W. 2010 (ed.), Levy A., & Menking W. 2012 (ed.), Patteeuw V., Vandeputte T., Van Gerrewey C. 2012 (ed.), Arrhenuis T., Lending M., Miller W., Mc Gowan J. M. 2014 (ed.)

one hand, aim to frame the architecture exhibition as a relevant event in the definition of possible histories of architecture (Cohen 1999), and on the other, see the exhibition as an instrument capable of disseminating the practice of building and architectural research (Sudjic 2008). Architecture exhibitions cover a wide spectrum of activities that include a variety of curatorial positions and authorial activities, as for example, architecture exhibition model settlements realised for international exhibitions, shows of architectural drawings, public presentations of competition results, and even certain initiatives organised for celebrating the completion of a building (Chan 2010). To each one of these moments we can associate different ways of conceiving exhibition practices: architecture can be explained, documented, represented in abstract form, or interpreted.

The diffusion of architecture exhibition studies has certainly been fostered by the growing circulation, which began at the end of the seventies, of places, centres and institutions dedicated to the presentation of architecture[3]. The actual panorama of architecture exhibitions is more variegated than ever. In this we can identify two main fields to which architecture exhibitions belong: on one side we have architecture exhibitions whose aim is to document the built substance of an edifice (also when this cannot be displayed in the exhibition space because built elsewhere) through a variety

3 The DAM (Deutsches Architekturmuseum) was founded in Frankfurt in 1977, the CCA (Canadian Centre for Architecture) in 1979; also that same year the autonomy of architecture as a sector in the Venice Biennale was recognised and the ICAM (International Confederation of Architectural Museums) was established.

of elements ranging from those proper to architectural design, such as drawings and three-dimensional models (also in 1:1 scale), and extending to photography and video; on the other side we observe the diffusion of exhibition forms in which the object of the show is not so much the architecture itself but the social, economic, cultural and artistic backgrounds that have led to the project's formation and to the possible realisation of architecture. In shows such as these the forms of representation extend beyond those commonly used to exemplify objects which could potentially be built or which have already been built, and include forms and languages that traditionally do not belong to the world of architecture.

These issues open up an interesting area of investigation on the theme mainly because it is clear that the presentation of architecture in an exhibition through the conventional instruments of architectural representation will inevitably generate a divide between those presenting the works and those observing them. Conventionally, the public of an architectural show is expected to be able to interpret a code/language that is specific to the discipline (drawings and models originate as instruments for investigating the project and for building architecture more than for explaining it to the public). In addition to this, often times the instruments of architecture representation are invested with an *aura* that somehow draws them closer to the art world so much so that drawings are, at times, treated as if they were paintings, and three-dimensional models as if sculptures (Urbach 2010). However, if exhibitions exist whose aim is not so much to focus on the representational capacities of those who have produced the works on display, as it is to make a spatial experience available to the public, then various factors should be considered so that important issues are not neglected in the mediation process taking place within the exhibition space.

The structure of this book – The present text is the result of a study on the architecture exhibition carried out at the Faculty of Design and Art of the Free University of Bozen Bolzano. Its aim is to make a contribution to the present debate both by laying the foundation for mapping contemporary architecture exhibition practices and by attempting to identify the cultural and communication contexts in which they are positioned.

The aim of this book starts from the simple observation that if architecture defines the built realm that surrounds us, and is built in order to be inhabited (in the countless ways in which the word *inhabited* can be interpreted) by each one of us, then it seems contradictory that, in the collective consciousness, architecture exhibitions almost exclusively address an expert audience. It was my objective to identify which approaches, and how many, are best capable of expanding the panorama to include further and significant forms that the architecture exhibition may acquire. The purpose was not to investigate the possibility of heightening an indistinct public's enjoyment of those exhibitions, but to concentrate on the contents of the exhibitions themselves, on the devices adopted in the communication practices employed therein, and on the possible relations with the public so as to highlight characteristics and meanings. This book collects contributions that focus on the pressure of radical transformation to

which the architecture exhibition is actually subjected. The writings do not come exclusively from scholars who have, with an attentive eye to external factors, examined the phenomenon of exhibiting architecture, but also from individuals directly involved in realising exhibition spaces, as curators, and in their production, as designers asked to give a tangible and inhabitable form to the show. Without lingering on the historical framework of the phenomenon of the architecture exhibition or on relevant case studies from the past, the work concentrates on contemporary practices in order to deliver an overview of the current situation.
The book is organised into two sections titled *The exhibition space as a field of action* and *On the side of the public*. The issues debated in the first section start with the questions, the criteria, and the considerations that animate a curator in the developing of an exhibition and extend to the relationships that exist between the exhibited content and the instruments and devices utilised for its presentation. The contributions in this book make room for the decisions taken regarding exhibiting and for the possible perspectives on the built realm which might be considered relevant for the transmission of information that occurs in the exhibition space. Based on the assumption that also in the architecture exhibition the space is organised in order to generate communication, the book takes into account numerous aspects which help to define the added value of a general knowledge on architecture or on an architectural idea being diffused via the exhibition, compared to what otherwise would happen through other vehicles like, for example, publications. In the second part of the volume the focus is directed toward the architec-

ture exhibition public, with particular attention to the different types of visitors the exhibition addresses and to the relationships and dependencies that are generated between the exhibition content, the form chosen for exhibiting, and the observers. The section contains some significant examples of exhibitions that distance themselves from the notion shared by the public concerning this issue, allowing instead for an immersion, a spatial engagement capable of generating a personal relation between visitor and exhibition content. Furthermore, this section takes into consideration the meaning that spatial organisation has for transmitting content in other exhibiting contexts, such as the art exhibition.

The two interviews contained in this publication – respectively with Kersten Geers from OFFICE Kersten Geers David Van Severen and with Maarten Gielen from ROTOR – are closely tied to the chapters they follow, while simultaneously opening up cross references and defining possible intersections with other contributions in the volume when considered in its entirety. Possible keys to reading the text are highlighted through analogy and contrast. OFFICE Kersten Geers David Van Severen and ROTOR have recently realised important architecture exhibitions. The two interviews focus on two works in particular: the exhibition *7 Rooms, 21 Perspectives* at the Architecture Biennale 2010 by OFFICE Kersten Geers David Van Severen, and the Architecture Triennale in Oslo *Behind the Green Door. Architecture and the Desire for Sustainability,* which took place in 2013, by ROTOR.
7 Rooms, 21 Perspectives is a contemplative space.

In this exhibition the two architects concentrate on the forms of representation of architecture in an exhibition context and stage a coherent dialogue between images and interventions in real scale, investigating the constructive power of photography both in the erection of architecture as well as in the configuration of the space itself. References abound and are not simply interferential but also allude to other episodes where OFFICE Kersten Geers David Van Severen has dialogued with the public through exhibit interventions, as in the case of the exhibition *7 Rooms* at the De Singel in Antwerp (indeed the Venetian show is basically a *re-enactment* of the Antwerp show). The photographs by Bas Princen relate with the exhibition space and with the collages and the three-dimensional interventions conceived *in situ* (which, in turn, can be considered as a sort of spatial collage). The topic of the intervention in scale 1:1 is strongly present in the interview and resumes many of the issues dealt with in the other contributions in the book, one such example being the text by Wilfried Kuehn, which vehemently debates this subject. What is particularly interesting to underline, to this end, is how the 1:1 interventions in the Venetian show are neither reproductions or *mise en scène* of projects, nor are they devices supporting the presented objects. They are instead, in every respect, constructive elements that render the space of the exhibition inhabitable. They are the content of the exhibition, and not interventions functional to its fruition. After all, an incisive attitude towards the exhibition of architecture – as is argued in the interview – already appeared in *After the Party,* presented by OFFICE Kersten Geers David Van Severen during the Architecture Biennale 2008, in which, as in a sort of manifesto, the pointlessness of the documentation in architecture exhibitions was openly ceclared. In regards to the use of photography, there emerges in the interview an interpretation of this means of expression not so much as a representational tool but as an instrument of enquiry – an enquiry necessary for the construction of the space as a founding element of the very project.

The border between the project of a space and the exhibiting of its design is definitively dismantled. "Perspective", "framing" and "cutting" (utilised also by Bas Princen in his images) are expressly pointed out as design elements of architecture, not of its representation: this is an approach that resonates with what Anne Holtrop argues in his contribution *Openness*.

Behind the Green Door is a discursive space. In their practice, ROTOR distance themselves from what they define as a "stereotypical architecture exhibition" and establish a relation with that category of exhibition events in which the architectural production is presented as an issue within broader critical contexts and acquires a central role from points of view that are at times unexpected, yet extensively described, as, for example in Giovanna Borasi's contribution. ROTOR do not wish to talk exclusively about architecture; they prefer to use architecture in order to talk about something else that happens around it. The exhibition described by ROTOR is not monographic, but rather a research process concerned with an issue that becomes the subject of the exhibition. In the work of ROTOR criteria and sequences are subverted and the very construction process of the exhibition space becomes show. The theme of real scale intervention resurfaces, but the visitor is not compared with a reproduction in scale 1:1 of something outside of the exhibition, rather he or she is invited to inhabit a model in real scale. The immersive experience in this model becomes the exhibition itself. From a curatorial point of view, *Behind the Green Door* is not an exhibition that aims to confirm the statement of a curator but an instrument through which he or she addresses the visitor in a critical way, asking a series of questions that may be answered in different ways. The role of the visitor within the exhibition is essential and this is confirmed by the activation of the exhibition space through a series of guided tours that are part of a programme integrated into the exhibition which directly includes the public in the presented subject.

The book closes with a transcription made of Tina di Carlo's contribution to the conference *Displayed Spaces*, organised in March 2013 at the Faculty of Design and Art of the Free University of Bozen Bolzano and in the context of the research project that led to the realisation of this book. The passage reiterates the words with which Tina di Carlo opened the day. Her questions are intentionally put at the end of this publication and resonate with, as well as amplify, the discussion. What remains after the exhibition? What traces does it leave? What is more important: the experience of an ephemeral phenomenon such as an exhibition or the echo that such an exhibition is able to produce in the public opinion, in the debate on architecture and in its history?

References

Arrhenuis T., Lending M., Miller W., Mc Gowan J. M. (ed.) (2014), *Place and Displacement, Exhibiting Architecture,* Zürich, Lars Müller Publishers.

Bois Y.-A., Hollier D., Krauss R. (1999), A conversation with Jean-Louis Cohen, *October 89,* October Magazine, Ltd. and Massachussets Institute of Technology, pp. 3-18

Chan C. (2010), *Exhibiting Architecture: Show don't tell,* www.domusweb.it/it/architecture/esporre-larchitettura-illustra-non-parlare [11/11/2014]

Cohen J.-L. (1999), Exhibitionist Revisionism. Exposing Architectural History, *JSAH vol. 58 nr. 3 – Architectural History 1999/2000,* pp. 316-325

den Oudsten F. (2012), The Poetry of Place, Kossmann, H., Mulder, S., den Oudsten, F., *Narrative Spaces,* 010 Publishers, Rotterdam, pp. 8-30

Di Carlo T. (ed.) (2010), *Log20, Curating Architecture*

Levy A. & Menking W. (2010), *Architecture on display: on the history of the Venice Biennale of Architecture,* London, Architectural Association Publications

Levy A., & Menking W. (2012), *Four Conversations on the architecture of discourse,* London, Architectural Association Publications

Patteeuw V., Vandeputte T., Van Gerrewey C. (ed.) (2012), *OASE 88, Exhibitions. Showing and Producing Architecture.* Rotterdam, 010 Publishers

Sudjic D. (2008), Introduction, Sparke P., Sudjic D., *Representing Architecture. New discussions: ideologies, techniques, curation,* London Design Museum, pp. 16-31

Urbach H. (2010), Exhibition as Atmosphere, Di Carlo T. (ed.), *Log20, Curating Architecture,* pp. 11-17

Zardini M. (2012), A project for two buildings, *icam print 04,* pp. 30-35

THE SPACE OF THE EXHIBITION AS A FIELD OF ACTION

When we work on architecture exhibitions, we should linger on their meaning and ask ourselves what we exhibit when we present the built realm or issues incident to this in the context of a show and, above all, we should ask ourselves why we exhibit. In recent years, and slightly behind that which has already happened in the art world, the space of the exhibition has increasingly become a field of action in which objects of different nature are brought to dialogue with the space that hosts them; a space of intense debate on the meaning of exhibiting, and one of reflection on the multiple roles that this space can acquire in the construction of a shared knowledge around architecture. This very issue probably contains one of the most complex and interesting elements of the object of study documented by this volume: the architecture exhibition is space showing space. Architecture exhibitions, as well as all other forms of exhibition, generate communication. The contributions presented here focus on the added value represented by the diffusion of knowledge about architecture or, in a broader way, the diffusion of an idea *of* architecture or *on* architecture through this tool. They define a variegated reasoning on the contemporary practices of exhibiting architecture and on the context in which such practices are implemented. Giovanna Borasi gives a very clear statement on the significance of the architectural show and on its nature as a strategic tool capable of fostering the debate on architecture as well as on issues that are relevant to it. Through a lucid line of thinking, the exhibition is described not so much as an instrument of representation but as an opportunity to investigate and reflect.

The approach put forward is that of the Canadian Centre for Architecture (CCA) in Montréal, an institution where Giovanna Borasi works as a chief curator and for which she curated and co-curated several exhibitions in the past. The projects presented are characterised by an undeniable narrative component. In them exhibition and display are an essential component of the curatorial strategies and contribute to the interpretation of the objects in the exhibition space. Giovanna Borasi contextualises the question, which always recurs in the discourse around architecture exhibitions, of the absence of the object building in the exhibition, harking back to a possible weakness of the presented substitutes and concentrating on the practices that put these into dialogue with the exhibition space that is thus activated. The exhibited objects are transformed and reinvented and these operations – necessary for generating resonance – become founding elements of a curatorial practice, ones which should not be closed up in a specialised domain but left as open as possible. Anne Holtrop scrutinises the border between the production of the space and its representation in the exhibition context and openly confesses his scepticism towards a clear distinction between the two worlds of art and of architecture. Talking about his own work he quotes *Opera Aperta,* in which Umberto Eco refers to the decision of the artist to make space for the presence of the public and for the unforeseen during the moment of fruition. In Holtrop's words we recognise the importance ascribed to understanding that seeing architecture in its model state can supply answers and can help us concentrate on focuses that are completely different from what happens when we stand in front of

a realised building. This is the starting point for a very personal approach based on the conviction that architecture and its exhibition should not necessarily be seen as two distinct identities. Everything is architecture; therefore also the public moment in which observer and object meet in the exhibition space does not represent something that is somewhere else.
Anne Holtrop exhibits contexts that are strongly marked by a peculiar sensibility for the *here and now:* the intervention in the museum and the exhibited work are exactly the same. A further level of complexity can be added to all this: it is outlined by references and photographic representations in which the photographs sometimes represent *other* spaces, sometimes the very objects that are present in the exhibition. Their aim is not to represent architecture in order to bring it into the exhibition space but instead to found basic elements of the exhibition experience. This supplies a double perception of places which, in the end, are exactly the same: once from the point of view of the photography and once from the point of view of the construction of its model. Objects and photography, although different and discrepant in their materiality, are put close together in open compositions linked by a common story to tell: as Anne Holtrop says, a story of space and architecture.
Wilfried Kuehn starts his contribution from the premise that architecture is always exhibited and that it is unnecessary to transfer it into an exhibition space. The position rises from a personal mistrust towards the museum and the restrictive aspects related to the transmission of knowledge through exhibitions. Architecture and exhibition are interpreted as two

words which cannot be separated from one other; to this he adds reflections on the real scale – the 1:1 – that start from architectural interventions of a pronounced *exhibitionist* character and extend to emotional and physical experiences within the exhibition itself. The observations on the space of the exhibited objects are intended as a relational issue that is not purely geometrical, thus the architecture show is interpreted as a tool capable of framing and opening reality to other possible points of view. For Wilfried Kuehn there is a purely conceptual dimension to architecture and its exhibition, a dimension that he tried to practice, for example, by asking the artist Armin Linke to collaborate on the curation of the *Carlo Mollino – Maniera Moderna* exhibition in the interest of a *curatorial design* that foresees also, and above all, an intense relation between concept and authoriality.

FOR ARCHITECTURE

Giovanna Borasi

Is the exhibition of architecture of *or* about *or* for *architecture? This simple question challenges the idea of what an exhibition is and furthermore what its content is, the modality adopted to construct it, its public, and ultimately its scope. Is the exhibition an objective* per se, *or a strategic tool among others to foster ideas, challenge positions, introduce new themes, question current topics in the attempt to ultimately advance new theories and change current practices? The role of a curator, together with that of an institution, is then, in this new framework, radically different from the conventional one. More similar to the process of defining an architectural project, the curator advances, through the use of different tools (exhibitions, books, microsites…), a complex set of ideas not only* about *architecture but* for *architecture. If today we can now say that for the artist the role of being a creator, of being something new and original is over – since an artist now works more in a condition that could be described by strategies of remix, copy-paste, collage, quotations and montage – just as we can say the same for those working in the curatorial practice as a form of cultural production, then a possible strategy for defining the curator's new role could be that of appropriation, of selecting, transforming and combining to produce new perspectives for architecture, where the curator is transformed into an exhibition auteur and a creator himself. Through the ongoing research at the Canadian Centre for Architecture (CCA), which strives to find a strategy towards establishing a curatorial voice, I will illustrate just such a position.*

As a possible point of departure for illustrating the process of rethinking the way we operate at the Canadian Centre for Architecture (CCA), both as curators and as an institution, I would like to use an archival document in the form of a short video. It is an interview made in the 1970s by an English BBC journalist with Saudi Arabia's Minister for Petroleum and Mineral Resources at that time. This filmed interview was part of the exhibition *1973: Sorry Out of Gas,* curated by CCA Director Mirko Zardini and myself in 2007.

During that precise historical period a clear shift in

***1973: Sorry, Out of Gas*, installation view, 2008.**

global power was taking place, both in terms of geography and economy: the countries which were then considered as developed, found themselves faced with a challenging situation; due to the oil embargo they could not rely on cheap and easily accessible energy any longer. In the interview the journalist, Richard Kershaw, challenges the Arab Minister, Sheikh Ahmed Zaki Yamani, arguing that the Arab producers cannot raise the oil price as they wish since this action will have a heavy impact on their economy and growth; the Minister responds by asking why Western countries are always the ones to define the rules, and invites instead the interviewer (together with all developed countries) to adjust their ideas and their approach to this new condition. Indeed this new condition was to establish the beginning of a new era.

The video could be understood as a metaphorical illustration to the approach that the CCA is using today in the conception of its exhibitions. In response to the various types of crises we have faced in the last ten years (ecological, financial, social, etc.), the CCA's direction could be read as an attempt at contributing in an active way to the contemporary debate, introducing a different idea of curating, together with a new role for the museum.

Exhibitions as means of thematic explorations

With the aim of continuously rethinking our disciplines and the boundaries of our field of study, at the CCA we decided to question and re-examine the assumption of how architects operate today. We embarked on a study and revision of assumptions, preconceptions and attitudes in the field, revealing unexamined facets and hidden agendas to these issues. Through a careful selection of topics and themes we argue that a series of exhibitions could become a way to initiate and contribute to the contemporary debate related to these issues. Ideas on perception, landscape, ecology, energy, lifestyle, activism, migration, the future, progress, and health have all found their way into the CCA exhibitions, creating a thematic system of exploration.
These exhibitions have allowed us, as Mirko Zardini argued in his essay *A project for Two Buildings* (2012), to investigate the grey zone at the crossroads of contemporary culture, society and architecture and to critically expose its contradictions. The thematic approach also acknowledges the necessity of injecting the discourse of architecture, city landscape and environment into a broader context, to show how they are interwoven with our daily lives, what they are responsible for and how they can contribute to defining problems and improving the search for possible solutions.

The transformation of exhibitions into the exploration of themes and emerging problems in an attempt to suggest a different role for architecture and planning today, with the consequence of moving away from solely monographic shows, is one of CCA's many responses to the current context. With this new thematic perspective we are able to connect architecture to the context in which it was produced. This approach offers visitors a means of visualizing and appreciating the materials presented, but also exposes them to potential problems, new discourses and fresh perspectives.
Finally, this way of conceiving exhibitions might allow for, or even require, the construction of a different platform for contemporary architecture to work upon. In this sense the CCA's ambition may stretch even beyond the series of thematic shows we have produced

at the CCA over the last decade. It involves the idea of contributing to the future by revealing or pointing out a current issue and bringing forth the specific cultural agenda related to it: as if an exhibition of contemporary architecture could anticipate, as it happens with great architecture, what is to come, responding not only to what is needed but preparing a platform from which planners, architects and designers could then work.

Exhibitions *for* architecture

This work and research has also implied a strategic change in the conception of the meaning and scope of an exhibition. Is it an architecture exhibition *of* architecture, *about* architecture, *on* architecture or *for* architecture? This simple question challenges the idea of what an architecture exhibition is for, what its content and the modality adopted to construct its public are, as well as, ultimately, what its scope is. At the CCA we have been shifting our attention from exhibition *of*, *on* and *about* architecture to exhibitions *for* architecture.

These exhibitions could be understood as "promises of architecture" (Zardini, 2011). The role of the curator together with that of the institution is, in this new framework, radically different than that of the traditional one. The institution thus plays an active role in this new scenario, as it selects the themes to explore as the important issues deserving attention and reflection. Similar to the process put in place by an architectural practice in designing an architectural project, the curator actively advances, through a set of different tools (exhibition, book, website), a complex set of ideas not only *about* architecture but *for* architecture. The curatorial practice with its set of different tools, becomes then a way to produce ideas on architecture that contribute to the current discourse and introduce new forms of dialogue through the figures of architects, urban planners, landscape architects and designers. A thematic exhibition could in fact also become a place where architects, unknown to or unfamiliar with one another, could meet and confront ideas. Indeed the curatorial practice evolves in a similar manner to the process an architect undertakes when building a project, or that of a writer when writing a book, or a film director when making a movie. A decade ago curator and writer Jens Hoffmann was already acknowledging and foreseeing this change in the curatorial role:

> The curators are turning themselves from simple exhibition organizers into exhibition auteurs and creators. When we look just a few decades back, the curator was someone who would quite anonymously organize an exhibition in a museum or another form of art institution in rather conventional terms. During the second half of the 20th century, curators began to emancipate themselves from being purely the custodians of museum collections or the administrative organizers of exhibitions. They began to articulate a particular form of creativity in the organization of exhibitions, which were increasingly based on particular themes or other over-arching curatorial concepts. From Harald Szeemann to Hans Ulrich Obrist this chapter came to a close towards the end of the 1990s when a more differentiated and complex notion of curating emerged. Today many curators display a thematic consistency in their work and despite the long proclaimed death of the author they are being compared more and more with authors who would demonstrate an artistic development through time, creating an oeuvre not unlike a film director, a writer or a visual artist.
> Over the last decades, a diversity of curatorial approaches has helped to make this emancipation possible and we have never seen more variation in curatorial models. (Hoffmann, 2005)

This change in the role of the curator reinforces this stand that considers an exhibition not merely an objective *per se* but rather a strategic tool, among other possible ones, for fostering ideas, challenging positions, introducing new themes, questioning current topics and, ultimately, for advancing new theories and changing current practices; that the objective of an exhibition is not to document the absent work, but to propose the ideas of potential architectures, their relationship to the surrounding world, and the shaping of thought through exhibiting.

Appropriation as curatorial modality

However, if we consider the curator as an author, then what kind of model or modality can the curator propose or adopt? In recent years we assisted in the diffusion of a great number of writings and publications on what it is *to be a curator.* These publications have revealed a current interest in the specific figure and role of the curator: somehow they help us to clarify and better understand the possible landscape in which the curator could move and even expand his/her expertise. Also helping the expansion of the curatorial field is the relatively new phenomenon of the emergence of a fairly large number of new curatorial programmes offered by universities, museums and other cultural institutions. Do these new activities somehow constitute an attempt at defining a new field of expertise? The risk implied in this approach is to confine curatorship to a specialist domain, while it may instead benefit to keep it as open a field as possible. Curators with a variety of backgrounds (e.g. in history, architecture, journalism, art) have, therefore, a multitude of approaches, so that even if a person is not doing this as a profession, he/she could easily make incursions into the field. If we accept the thesis that the artist's role of being a creator of something new and original is over, that an artist now works more in a contemporary condition that can easily be described as a strategy of remix, copy-paste, collage, quotation and montage for a curatorial practice understood as a form of cultural production, then a possible strategy to adopt is that of *appropriation:* selecting, transforming and combining to produce new perspectives *for* architecture. Here again the curator is transformed into an author, a kind of *selective appropriator.* After all, since the nucleus of curating is still based on a filtering mechanism, the curator has to appropriate in order to oversee, contextualise, organise and administer.

A simple and perhaps somewhat extreme example of this approach is the Museum of Innocence established by Orhan Pamuk in Istanbul a few years ago. Pamuk translated his novel of the same name, *The Museum of*

1973: Sorry, Out of Gas, installation view, 2008.

Pulling a structure across the ice to Conche, Newfoundland, Canada, 1965.

Journeys: How travelling fruit, ideas and buildings rearrange our environment, installation view, 2010.

Innocence (2009), into a real space, one built upon his thoughts and words, which we can now experience. In order to do that he selected, appropriated, composed and, most of the time, invented a series of objects that can tell and narrate his story.

The exhibition I organised and curated at the CCA in 2011 entitled *Journeys: How Travelling Fruits, Ideas and Buildings Rearrange our Environment* could also be seen as an example of this approach. The exhibition investigated the topic of migration and the circulation of ideas about architecture, techniques of construction, planning strategies, expertise and architectural types – all significant things that move from one place to another because of people moving and bringing them along.

As the topic is an extremely vast one, and as migration is often linked to a specific and personal human story, I proposed selecting fifteen stories and facts which took place in the last century in different places and involving either an entire region or just several people. Appropriating narratives, personal histories and specific facts was a way to elaborate and recall these stories both in the exhibition and in the accompanying book.

These particular stories were also selected to bring to life a more general issue: how architectural ideas or ways of building and farming migrate from one place to another, and in so doing inform the built environment.

But if a book could easily sustain a story, a narrative, or even fiction, how do we transfer this approach into the gallery? The idea was to select for each case a few objects as witnesses of that particular story, in an attempt to sustain our perspective. For example, one story focused on the transformation of the Bijlmermeer neighbourhood in Amsterdam – after the Dutch government offered Dutch passports to Suriname citizens – from the modern idea of social housing to a problematic ghetto due to the waves of incoming/outgoing migrants. This led to a project by OMA in 1986 and to several subsequent ones. In this case, in addition to architectural material, important newspaper clippings and video footage were found in local archives which helped trace the change in how the neighborhood was inhabited over time. Another example is that of the fascinating story of an entire area

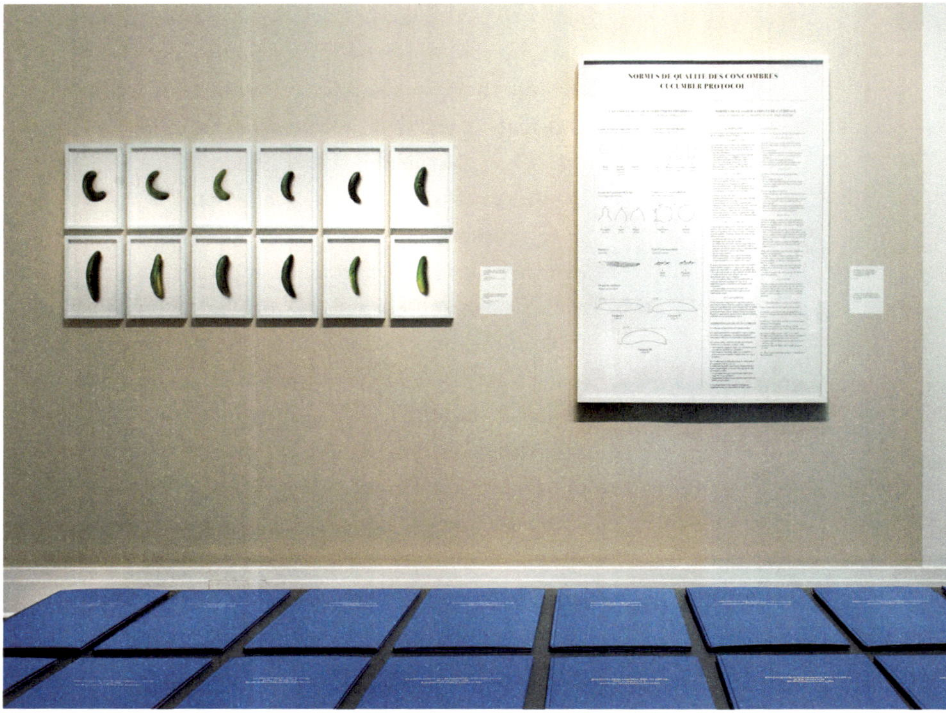

***Journeys: How travelling fruit, ideas and buildings rearrange our environment*, installation view, 2010.**

in the Canadian province of Newfoundland, where it was decided in the 1950s to relocate 30,000 people. Since the houses in the region were traditionally built to be moved along the coast according to the economic needs of the community, the people also relocated along with their own homes. A very emotional documentary film made by the Canadian National Film Board was presented in the exhibition to show how the houses were moved for kilometres and kilometres over the water or the ice.

In this exhibition my approach was similar to that of archeologists or forensic experts: we rebuilt or put together something that took place in the past with only a few clues and objects to help us. However, we did not have the actual objects for all of the stories. So we decided to invent and (re)produce some of them in an attempt to help the visitor reconstruct the specific story. This approach could be exemplified by the section of the exhibition that illustrated the absurd EU-law (compiled in all the official languages of the European community) that regulates the production and trade of vegetables, such as cucumbers: the only way we had of rebuilding and

visualising this story was to reconstruct the bureaucratic atmosphere of an office with the regulation printed in cahiers of European blue colour and a series of pictures of the different shapes of the cucumbers so as to emulate the idea of a Lombroso approach to physical defects.
These cultural objects were produced inside the museum as new original materials, as necessary objects to sustain and visualise the curatorial narrative. The general narrative, based on the fifteen selected stories, was then deployed in the gallery space following the conceptual design by artist Martin Beck and based on the idea of creating a specific atmosphere for each story. The visitor was left to connect the different stories, using these cultural objects as points of contact along the narrative.

An exhibition is thus intended as a scenario, a kind of post-production that from time to time creates a particular context for the presentation of cultural objects in a physical space. This path certainly allows for an original space to be created in the discourse of architecture, but it is also an approach that calls for critique. However, I would argue that this approach is not different from that of the architect which appropriates, combines, remixes, and quotes the work of past architects and artists to develop his own new thoughts.
This approach has been challenging, even for us inside the institution. Many of the objects we exhibit, especially if not from the CCA collection, have a kind of strange status: they are not necessarily art pieces and some of them are even copied or re-enacted objects. There is not even an institutional system in place yet to refer to them in order to insert/add them in our database because they do not fall under the traditional definition of collection objects. This rationale is, nonetheless, driven by a strong idea of selection: in an exhibition the choice falls always on the object which the curator reputes as the right one for supporting the idea he wants to convey. In this sense, this might be the era in which the curator becomes an author himself, the *creator* of the cultural object. It is a challenging operation in a museum environment: it is a new object, it is not collectible and still it becomes an object in the exhibition, presented along with the originals.

Imperfect Health: The Medicalization of Architecture, installation view with *Cow, Pig* and *Chicken* by Andy Byers, 2011.

One of the most recent shows I worked on at the CCA is *Imperfect Health: The Medicalization of Architecture.* The show and the related book challenge the role of architecture, landscape and urbanism in relation to contemporary issues of health. Today, anxiety over food, safety, smog, obesity, ageing and ground pollution and the perception that everything around us could be understood as a possible source of disease is leading to an obsession with the defense and fortification of the body. Medical sociologist Peter Conrad speaks about the process of medicalization of our society (2007). Things that once were not considered as illnesses (like obesity and alcoholism), are now considered so.

Medicalization is a process in which ordinary problems are described in medical terms and understood through a medical framework. Design is also affected by such anxieties and what we are observing today is that architecture is going through the same process, that is, looking for justification of its existence and waiting to have a crucial role in our society, as well as waiting to become a helpful and necessary player in finding a cure. *Imperfect Health* brings to life certain contradictions: Could design and architecture really be the cure for such issues? Do we really know what is healthy for us and could architecture give that to us? Is the role of architecture to concern itself with health matters or to find an ultimate cure? Why is architecture taking a bellicose stand, typical of western medicine, to combat illness, stress and viruses instead of taking other attitudes such as listening? We wanted to transfer these kinds of questions and the ambiguity of all possible answers to the visitors, keeping them in a continuous state of questioning, while understanding the complexity of the topic. To do this we selected and appropriated architect's ideas, or what we read as the main concept of their projects, we displayed the work of photographers, and we commissioned new pieces in an attempt to convey to the visitor where, in our opinion, architecture stands today on health issues. Objects, photos, models and drawings were displayed in order to create the oppositional characters that we decided to assign them in our plot (the exhibition design by Kersten Geers and David Van Severen

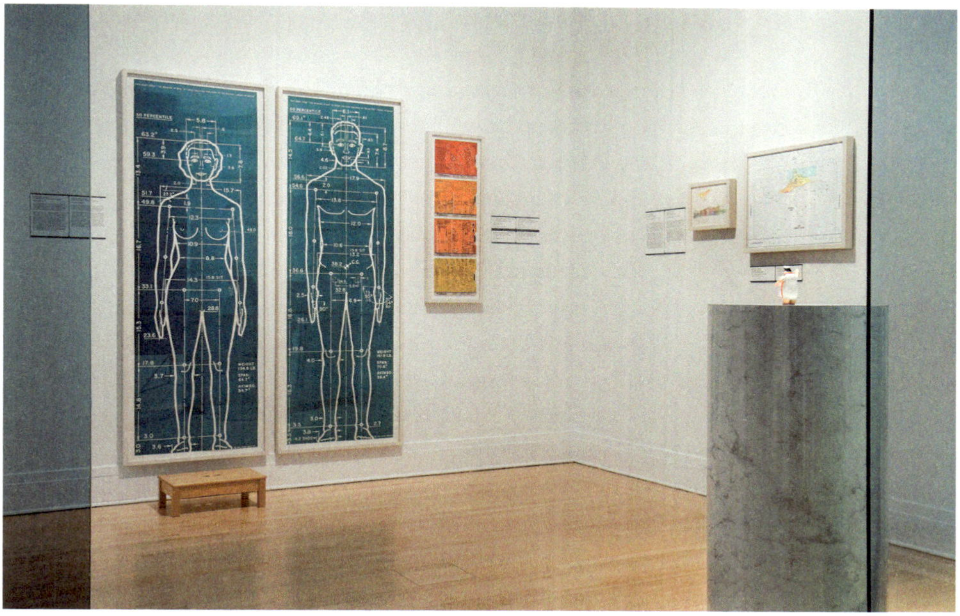

Imperfect Health: The Medicalization of Architecture, installation view, 2011.

reinforced this confrontational ambiguity of the objects' status). In choosing to do this we made all the objects have this kind of ambiguity (for example: a photograph of a place to which one goes to recover from asthma that looks scary, as if it were a bomb shelter; pictures of a beautiful landscape that is actually an asbestos mine; a version of the *Rabbit* chairs by Kazuyo Sejima and Ryue Nishizawa, enlarged and stretched in comparison to the original ones, designed expressly for the New Museum in New York as a way to represent the change of body sizes between Japan and North America). Many objects were displayed in the exhibition and even if the topic was taken absolutely seriously – and this is part of the CCA strategy – we always tried to add a trace of irony. This approach is evident for example in the particular selection of photographs of Sun City: a city for ageing people, in which you can live only if you are over fifty-five, and where everything is made of plastic so you don't have to worry about injuring yourself even on your lawn. Someone could argue we appropriated and *used* these projects and ideas to sustain our overall curatorial idea. It is indeed a way of curating.

As Orhan Pamuk did for his Museum in Istanbul, I attempted also to compile a sort of *humble manifesto* about curating (Pamuk, 2012). A list of things that for me are related to curating or to curating in this specific way – take it as a draft and as a document to use for discussion:

- **The exhibition is a tool, not an objective.**
- **Conceive the exhibition *for* architecture and not *of*, *about*, or *on* architecture.**
- **Pick a topic.**
- **Reflect on a sequence of topics.**
- **Discuss grey zones of the contemporary.**
- **Use display as a curating device.**
- **Gather objects, surrogates, ad hoc new objects to sustain your ideas.**
- **Conceive the exhibition as a place and a platform to initiate discussion.**

In this new understanding of the role of an architecture exhibition the display becomes a crucial part of the

Actions: What You Can Do With the City, **installation view, 2008.**

exhibition. If in a traditional exhibition the display considers the relations between the materials in the show, in the case of an exhibition *for* architecture the setting is what takes on a significant role. The design becomes an integral part of the curatorial strategy, it participates in the interpretation of the objects in the gallery and in the narrative, and along the process it contributes to a better definition of the scope of the show and to the construction of a precise point of view. Finally, design determines the overall character and the atmosphere of the exhibition, establishing which way it will be read and the impression that the visitor will have. At the CCA, for each exhibition, we work with a different architect and a different graphic designer or other professional that we think will be important to have as a member of the team.

Architecture will always be somewhere else: in the city, in the landscape, but never in an exhibition. In the exhibition there is only room for its surrogate.
The surrogate not only defines what precedes the work, but it also comments on or describes what comes after it. It explains something that is not there it often happens that the surrogate is not even visually compelling or

Actions: What You Can Do With the City, installation view, 2008.

ALL-OUT FOOD PRODUCTION
A CALL TO ACTION!
DES VÉLOS PLANTENT DES JARDINS DE GUERRE
BICYCLE PLANTS WARTIME GARDENS

***Actions: What You Can Do With the City*, installation view, 2008.**

has no particular aura. So how does one deal with that? A drawing, dry or technical, a photocopy of a text or a sketch on a napkin... any of these things could contribute to a particular and very interesting interpretation of the ideas of the author; although they might be extremely weak and not visually compelling at first glance, they may be the right ones to convey a curatorial direction. The show *Actions: What You Can Do With the City,* which I co-curated with Mirko Zardini in 2008, is a good example of this challenge. We had many ephemeral objects or non-museum objects (such as a paper horse head used as a tool for the participatory design phase of a public park, used shoes, marmalade jars, bags of manure...): all these objects were fundamental for introducing the idea of a collection of very simple tools that anyone can produce and use. In our mind all these simple ideas as a whole became a provocative statement to rethink the process of planning with a completely new toolbox. So the real objects in the exhibition had to be reinvented or transformed in order to suit the museum environment and to convey the curatorial idea.

Curatorial practice goes far beyond amassing and organising cultural objects in a collection or producing exhibitions. I believe that the interesting aspect of

curating is how it operates at many levels. While curating you are shaping the contemporary debate because of the content, but especially because of the way you approach curating. It is an evolving field: it is like manipulating something that constantly changes in your hands.
Each time you curate an exhibition you operate on many aspects: you deliver content, and at the same time you define a way of curating, thus a different idea of thinking about the present.

References

Conrad P. (2007) *The medicalization of Society: On the Transformation of Human Conditions into Treatable Disorders,* Johns Hopkins University Press, Baltimore

Hoffmann J. (2005), *The Art of Curating and the Curating of Art,* transcript of lecture at NABA, Utopian Display http://www.theutopiandisplay.com/platform/the-art-of-curating-and-the-curating-of-art, [11/11/2014]

Pamuk O. (2008), *The museum of innocence,* Vintage International, New York

Pamuk O. (2012), *The Innocence of Objects,* Abrams Book, New York

Zardini M. (2011), Exhibitions and Promises of Architecture, *Lotus International – Interior Landscape* 146, pp. 89-96

Zardini M. (2012), A project for two buildings, *icam print 04,* pp. 30-35

OPENNESS

Anne Holtrop

I love accidents and unforeseen things. I like to experiment, without knowing where it will lead me. I am an architect.

In my practice I distinguish three types of work: one on buildings, one on temporary spaces and one on models and photos. All three are worked on more or less independently and within their own character. There is no hierarchy in relation to the different kinds of works. What the works share is what Umberto Eco called Opera Aperta, *the title of his book published in 1962 and translated in English as* The Open Work.
In this book he describes works of art, music, literature, architecture (only once) and poetry that deal with openness – that can be described as the artist's decision to leave arrangements of a work to the public or to chance. In the first chapter he writes: "Every reception of a work of art (read in this context: architecture) is both an interpretation and a performance of it, because in every reception the work takes on a fresh perspective for itself" (ibid.).
In this text, through my own work, I will position architecture in exhibitions as independent work that has the possibility to open itself up to the interpretation and the thoughts of its viewers and participants; an architecture that is receptive to a multiplicity of meanings, where its users must hunt and find – as indeed Eco says.

In my practice I distinguish three different kinds of works: the built works in a 1:1 scale, the temporary spaces, and the models. There is no hierarchy – they are all different fields where I work with architecture. For me the exhibition is not something where I re-present what I have already done, but a stage on which to represent new work, a step in my practice that can be done on many different levels. I wish to start with the built works because I consider myself an architect and not an exhibition designer or an artist.

Museum Fort Vechten,
Utrecht, Model A, 2011.

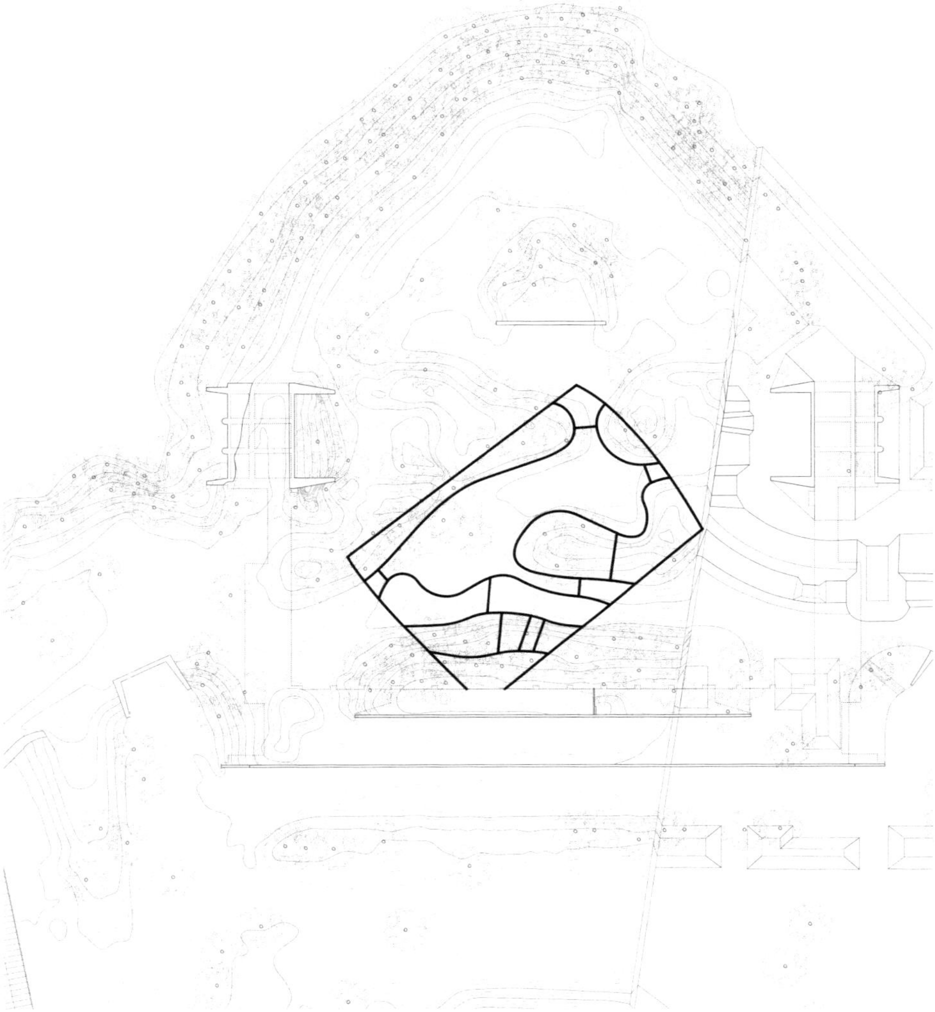

Museum Fort Vechten, Utrecht, Museum Mould, 2011.

Museum Fort Vechten, model, first prize invited competition, under construction, Utrecht (NL), 2011

During the 19th century the Dutch defence system was designed to flood large parts of the Netherlands in order to make the country inaccessible in case of assault. Fortresses were erected to defend the weakest points. The whole defence line will become an UNESCO monument. At one of the fifty-five fortress sites a museum will be built to explain the history. I was invited to participate in a competition.

Museum Fort Vechten,
Utrecht, Groundfloor, 2011.

Over the years the landscape of the fortresses eroded and turned into a Piranesian situation, where now and then architecture pops up. For the competition I obtained a plan of the museum site and worked on its present erosive state of the site, which at the beginning of the 19th century was perfectly intact. Nature had taken over and the site evolved into its current state. This gave me the idea for my proposal. I suggested to use for the form of the museum the exact same topographic contours just as they were in the map. In the project drawings the thick lines represent the walls of the museum. In a way I appropriate forms that are already there and use them for architecture. This is what I mean when I say that somehow everything you look at can also be considered architecture. It just depends on the way you look at it. As the model depicts, the building will be constructed under the ground level and will consist of a large and small patio which will help add light to the underground spaces. The large patio will also contain a large-scale model (50m long) of the whole waterline defence in the form of a relief on the floor. Visitors will be able to walk through the model and flood it by opening the locks.

Nine Photos for the exhibition Pictographs, curated by Valerio Olgiati, Venice Biennale (IT), 2012

This was an exhibition I took part in which was curated by Valerio Olgiati during the Venice Biennale for Architecture in 2012. Olgiati asked around forty architects from very different backgrounds and positions to contribute a maximum of ten images that were not about their own work but about their inspirations, their way of looking at architecture, or maybe about what influences them. What I found really interesting is the way he put the collected images on display, writing only the name of the architect on it – he did not explain anything. Famous names were invited and I found it interesting that you as a viewer had to interpret, since nothing was explained, what you were seeing. You might only recognise an architect's name amongst the images and the kind of stories they suggested. I liked this very much, this way of showing or talking about architecture. If you show things in this way, there is an *openness* of which the viewer can be a part. I feel it is very important that architecture is also displayed with this same kind of openness. To refer back to Umberto Eco's *Opera Aperta,* there is a very pleasing effect when you replace the word art with the word ***architecture:*** "...every reception of a work of *architecture* is both an interpretation and a performance of it, because in every reception the work takes on a fresh perspective for itself". One of the nine photos in my contribution for Olgiati's project is the picture of a leftover object in the studio where I was working in Tokyo. Even if this is about something that was never supposed to be architecture, you can start looking at it as a possible plan or a possible shape.

Pastoe 100 Years, felt pavilion and exhibition, exhibition made in collaboration with Krijn de Koning, Kunsthal Rotterdam (NL), 2012

Recently I completed the exhibition design of a show for Pastoe – a Dutch furniture brand that wanted to celebrate its centennial – in the Koolhaas Kunsthal in Rotterdam. As a concept behind the exhibition design I wanted to refer to Mies van der Rohe's *Wohnung unserer Zeit,* the German building exhibition of 1931. The Paolo Portoghesi Venice Architecture Biennale, which was architecture in action, was another interesting example I used for the exhibition's design concept. The space of the Kunsthal is 1,500 square metres and is so large that you can build a 1:1 architectural structure in it. Together with artist Krijn de Koning we proposed to construct three pavilions next to each other, equal in size but very different in their architecture and form. The middle one, the one I designed, was made completely in felt. The form has its origin from another exhibition on the De Stijl Movement that I did for the Gemeentemuseum in The Hague. The plan for the model, a three-dimensional typical De Stijl painting, was an arrangement of very small and very large spaces put together. For practical reasons we did not glue the model because we wanted to be able to easily change it, and when we got it back from the client all the spaces in the model were bent and twisted, pushing into each other and amazingly beautiful. It was something that you can only embrace. I made a drawing of its squeezed and

Contribution for the exhibition *Pictographs* by Valerio Olgiati, Venice Architecture Biennale 2012.

Like Pastoe, 100 years of design innovation, felt pavilion, installation view, Kunstal, Rotterdam, 2012.

Deformed model of the setting for the exhibition *Mondrian & De Stijl* at the Gemeentemuseum in The Hague, 2012.

bended spaces. It was an idea of architecture, but not on a built level; it existed only as a drawing and as a paper model that I made later. This is how I work. Most of the time I work without a commission and then there is this kind of stock of ideas, stock of interest in architecture, that somehow finds a way out once there is a commission. When there is a commission I do not start from zero, rather my interest already exists, and I establish a relation between the client and what I am doing. So, since that paper model had all these bended rooms, squeezed and deformed spaces, I thought felt would be a perfect material, a material that, I believe, already has gesture in itself, that can embrace an architectural idea. The architecture of the exhibition is completely made of one centimetre thick felt in a natural woollen colour. The spaces are shifted and deformed so, if what you normally see is the two sides of a wall, here the wall splits up and you see a multiplication of layers in the space.

I did the following three works together with Bas Princen.

Temporary Museum (Lake) and A Tower, model and photo diptych, in collaboration with Bas Princen, 2011

We showed these works, along with another two works, in the Centro Pecci in Prato in 2013. *Temporary Museum (Lake) and A Tower* consists of a diptych of two photos and a gypsum model. Both originated from other projects. The origin for the diptych was the project for a temporary museum in Heemskerk. I made a pavilion space for an art exhibition, a temporary space where artworks could be shown. The project was based on the pencil scribbles one makes during a phone call. Rapidly made drawings inspired by a work by Jean Arp called *dessin automatique,* which means things you do rather unconsciously, at least that was the argument at that time... Actually, I think that there is a great deal of consciousness in this work; I like the movement of the hand on the paper or the repetition of a certain kind of movement. I drew a complex, curvilinear squiggle along the paper, I took these forms and started interpreting them as possible plans for a building. It is interesting because the

Temporary Museum (Lake), **Heemskerk, drawing, 2010.**

form has already been given, but it has to be performed as architecture: what size that form will take, what I am looking at when I see the drawing, how I can move along this path or whether I need to access it at all.
Only half of the photo exists as a reality of the built space. In the diptych we doubled the space and put the two pictures in the corner of the exhibition space. The double photo suggests an endless interior. In contrast to this we placed this gypsum model next to the pictures. The model is solid and has as the museum a curvy perimeter. The model is solid, you can see it only from the outside.

A year before the Temporary Museum I completed a work named *A Tower* for an Art project space in Almelo, located in a tower and named 't Torentje. They wanted to celebrate their 20th anniversary, so I proposed a tower for the tower, very much inspired by Mies' Glass Skyscraper. For practical reasons I did not use real glass as Mies would have done. I decided to use mirror foil instead, because of the reflections and because mirror constantly dissolves when it reflects the night. I proposed it as a tower for apartments, one flat every level. For the work shown in Prato we translated the tower into a solid

Temporary Museum (Lake),
Heemskerk, drawing, 2010.

62

Temporary Museum (Lake),
Heemskerk, 2010.

Temporary Museum (Lake) and *A Tower,* model and photo diptych, Centro Pecci, Prato, 2013.

A Tower, installation view
't Torentje, Almelo, 2009.

form and it was amazing to see how the material could shift every point of view. Sometimes it could also be seen as a fragment of a gothic column. We placed the tower in front of the photo diptych in order to obtain an inside from which you cannot look out, and an outside from which you cannot look in. They each have a different materiality, so there is this further discrepancy between the two, but they tell a common story.

Batara, model and photos, in collaboration with Bas Princen, 2012

The third work, shown in Centro Pecci, is *Batara*. The project was centred around a trip to Petra, in Jordan, where Bas took a picture of the beautiful tombs dug into the mountains by the Nabataeans. The tombs remained undiscovered until the 19th century, when a Swiss archaeologist uncovered them. After the discovery they were dug up by archaeologists, in a similar way – by chiselling away material – to how the Nabataeans had sculpted them. If you walk along the mountains you can also see these places where the tombs were not so buried in the sand, and in that case time had eroded the landscape and given back to the stone a kind of natural state. What we both liked was that the architect did not construct, but rather made these beautiful constructions by taking away material. It is a kind of opposite way of working. We wanted to discover a sort of analogy and so I made a large sandbox in my studio where I started digging, taking away the sand and then casting the result with pigmented gypsum. On one side you have the rough side printed by the sand and on the flat side you have the pouring side. In this way there is an embedded relationship between natural and artificial. Afterwards I cut away parts from the forms so that the obtained objects could stand. I also cut a regular window where there was already a hole. In this way I obtained architectural elements, like walls and windows, and arranged them as if they were parts of a modern house in order to create spaces in-between.

While Bas and I were raising these walls we thought that they made sense and it would be interesting to show them together. At the same time Bas took photographs

Batara, element pouring, 2012.

of the arrangement: he placed the camera between the objects and took photos. We had the model as well and during the work we found out that this double perception of the space was the same thing, just seen once through photography and once through the model.
I think that this is very interesting because photography can diminish the fact that you always look from above when you look at a model from the outside. You can never really be part of a model. The model is a small scale exhibition space for the photos of this space. It links them up and makes continuous circles in this kind of exchange between these things.

Batara, installation view, Leth & Gori, Copenhagen, 2012.

Batara, installation view, Leth & Gori, Copenhagen, 2012.

Notes

When Pastoe asked Krjin de Koning and me to do the 100 years exhibition, they specifically did not want to hire an exhibition designer because they wanted to have a very independent spatial situation. They knew our practices and asked us, especially since the 1500 square metres of the Kunsthal was such a large space that just placing furniture in it would have resulted in that furniture simply disappearing. They liked the fact that they got from us a space, or a spatial situation, within which they could place their furniture. Hence from the client's question of what to do with this large space and small objects, the only thing we were certain we wanted to do was three different spatial situations; so we realised three very different pavilions: the first one is very minimal, abstract and completely painted in black; then we have the felt one; and thirdly a pavilion painted in very strong colours. It happened quite naturally that furniture fit in, almost as if the furniture pieces were in an existing space like a house. As Joseph Grima says (Vandeputte, 2012) these kinds of places, these kinds of exhibitions, are the perfect situation for experimenting with architecture, and I see the necessity of these places.

When I was in my last year of architecture school I asked Krijn de Koning to be one of my tutors because, to be honest, I always wanted to be an artist but I am an architect. You always walk around in order to find a position in which you feel confident: I like artists, I like their work and I like relating to them. One thing that I learned from Krjin is that when you design, you just have to start doing things without hesitating. That was for me an essential mental step. Firstly, I do not need to wait. Secondly, since I am an architect, I can consider everything I do to be architecture. These were the two very simple things that I learned from an artist, which gave the whole spin to my practice. This is the reason why I feel confident to make architecture now. I was always fighting against it because I did not like that everything in architecture should be about solutions to problems.

***Batara (Four Walls) Pavilion,* Rotterdam, 2013.**

The pavillion Batara was realised in the context of an exhibition called (Re)Sources which took place in WDW/ Rotterdam in 2013.

References

Eco U. (1989), The Poetics of the Open Work, *The Open Work,* translated by Anna Cancogni, Harvard University Press

Vandeputte T. (2012), Sites of Experimentation: In Conversation with Joseph Grima, *Oase 88,* pp. 62–67

1:1

Wilfried Kuehn

Space may be displayed but first of all space is a display itself. There is no architecture, which is not at once a display. If we address space as a relation rather than as a purely geometrical problem, we see our work as architects closely related to questions of exhibiting. Space needs to be experienced first-hand. Being itself invisible and untouchable, a space requires a 1:1 e perception-construction through subjective involvement. With the exhibition of architecture we are facing the doubling effect of this 1:1 experience. The way to display space then is making once more a different but equally real space. As we come to realise, 1:1 does not add up to exact repetition. Revisiting historical projects like Palladio's Teatro Olimpico and Ungers' Green Archipelago in this respect, we find evidence of the exhibition nature of architecture at varying scales. The key aspect of displayed space is the construction of a context which paradoxically rather than with the situation as found is to be identified with the architectural model to be inserted into it.
The theme is developed along projects by Kuehn Malvezzi like the competition for the Berlin Humboldt-Forum in 2008, the contribution to the Biennale di Venezia 2012 and the exhibition Carlo Mollino-Maniera Moderna at the Haus der Kunst Munich in 2011.

I'm going to approach the panorama that we are trying to embrace from a specific perspective. I am talking from the point of view of an architect, but I am also showing an exhibition that I co-curated because I think there are certain things happening between the curatorial and the design practices. In fact, these practices are not clearly separated. Design is not just a service that is delivered when one does an exhibition. Something is happening in-between and I will call it *curatorial design* because you may not decide if it is design or if it is curatorial practice when you make spatial decisions in exhibiting something.

Pediment

In Piero Manzoni's *Socle du Monde* the base displays the world as an object. The Earth became the object of an exhibition by way of being put on top and thus actually

Piero Manzoni, *Socle du Monde,* 1961.

under a pediment. Manzoni was engaging conceptually with an act of architecture: framing and opening the perceived reality to a different view. Manzoni's act does not change reality but triggers a different way to look at it. Thus the space of his exhibiting is not geometrical but rather relational: how we see and frame it, and this is what we call a display. The point is that this is not exhibition-architecture but architecture as such. Architecture always displays. Architecture is never just a building, architecture as space is not something that you can touch, it is not something that you can actually photograph and see but a reality you have to experience and thus produce yourself first hand. Space and architecture for that matter are always entities that are real, that are 1:1 and in their way they relate objects to one another because making architecture does not mean making a singular building but producing a context.
This principle guides our practice when we make architecture and we always think of how to make a 1:1 experience possible. 1:1 means life-sized in the sense of an unmediated experience. That is why I do not believe too much in scale models and in fact we talk a lot about models in our office but when we talk about models we think of models 1:1, we think of how reality itself becomes a model and assumes a demonstrative aspect by shifting your perspective. Manzoni actually made a model out of the Earth by displaying it.

Making things invisible

Le Corbusier, *Rooftop de Beisteguy,* Paris, 1929–31.

Charles de Beistegui, a Paris art collector and party animal of the 1920s, asked Le Corbusier to transform a rooftop on the Champs Elysees into a location that twenty years later might have been called a penthouse. Le Corbusier made moving hedges and a periscope through which you can look at Paris as an exhibition. He finally realised the *Plan Voisin* by way of display after no one would follow his plan to enhance Paris on the ground through physical demolition. With the help of these hedges put on top of the roof and the kind of wall the art collector himself had built (apparently with a fireplace), you could actually block out most of Paris and just look at what you wanted (which was the Arc de

Triomphe, in this case). The point is that Le Corbusier did not want to look at the whole city as a scenery but he wanted to display Paris as he conceptually imagined it: a void with singular monuments. In order to achieve this effect, he needed to reduce the visible reality. As we can see, exhibiting means making things invisible rather than visible.

Le Corbusier, *Pavillion de l'Esprit Nouveau*, Paris, 1925.

Cut-Out

The optical city model of the de Beistegui design goes back to another project Le Corbusier had done some years earlier, the Pavillon de l'Esprit Nouveau realised in 1925 for the International Decorative Arts Exhibition in Paris. The interesting part of this exhibition was the fact that Le Corbusier made a life size model of an apartment – the whole pavilion set in the park was actually a 1:1 cut-out of the *Immeuble-Villa* and you could walk in and look out from the apartment into the park, you were able to actually feel the whole experience of being in the *Immeuble-Villa* in spite of it not having been built. The point is again that it was part of an urban design scheme and, additionally, there was a big diorama inside of the pavilion, but still, as a visitor, you could directly experience its spatial reality.

Andrea Palladio, *Teatro Olimpico*, Vicenza, 1580–1585.

Palladio I

In the late 1500s Palladio realised in Vicenza his famous theatre, which is not a theatre at all but can be considered an exhibition. An exhibition of a theatre. This space is a display of the honour and dignity of the academy members who financed the project and it is basically a way of displaying the citizenship in Vicenza. It realises a *museification* of Roman architectural elements. It frames architecture; it is an architectural model that you can experience because its scenography creates an imaginary perspective behind the model of the Roman triumphal arch, the same way Le Corbusier framed the form of the Arc de Triomphe.

Canaletto, *Capriccio of Palladio buildings*, 1756–59.

Palladio II

Two Centuries after the theatre Canaletto paints the Palladio buildings as a Capriccio, putting them together in a sort of architecture museum, similarly to how the

Roman Villa Adriana in Tivoli or today's Pergamon Museum in Berlin were arranged. The almost complete work of Palladio is brought together in an imaginary architecture museum. Even this is a 1:1 model as it works through the experience of painting; thus rather than illustrating Palladio's architecture, Canaletto chose to transform it into yet another object of art.

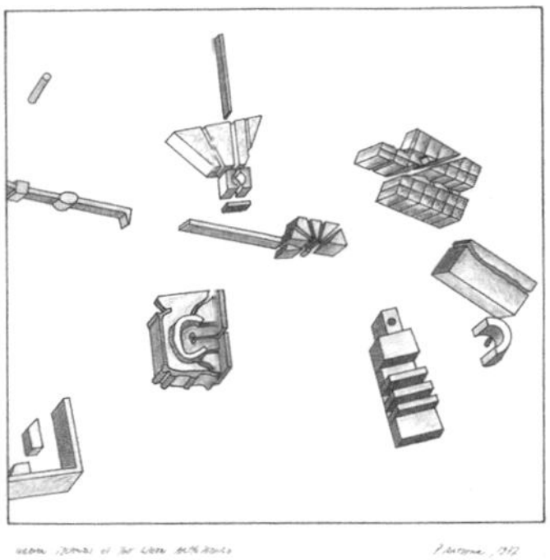

Oswald Mathias Ungers, *Berlin The Green Archipelago*, 1977.

Green Archipelago

In his 1977 drawing O. M. Ungers represents Berlin as a shrunken city that has been largely erased. Just isolated buildings remain like relics of a former age. This picture becomes an architectural museum not unlike the Capriccio by Canaletto. Ungers did in Berlin what Le Corbusier had done in Paris, although pointing more at morphological contexts than at singular buildings: He selected a limited number of architectural constellations, leaving out all the rest. Again, a show based not on amassing but on reducing. Reducing architecture and reframing it is the creation of a display. This example can be described as a form of urban design and can again be interpreted as a 1:1 exhibition.

Carlo Mollino, *Villa Garelli*, Champoluc, 1965.

Ready-Made

Villa Garelli in Champoluc, 1965. This building by Carlo Mollino is extremely interesting, because it is an architectural ready-made. Mollino did not invent this building, but he found it fifty kilometers away from where it stands now. The building, an old traditional hay barn in the rural valley, was dismantled and reassembled in Champoluc, on a new base built by Mollino. It is a base conceived to exhibit the old building and thus transform it from a barn into a villa. It is a very humble building put on display and made into something new. Mollino built in 1:1 scale something that he did not invent, but something that he reinvented through a different way of framing. He not so much created a building as he designed a context.

Modell Interconti

Martin Kippenberger, *Modell Interconti*, 1987.

It looks like a table but it actually is an artwork used as a ready-made to make yet another artwork. In 1987 Martin Kippenberger bought a 1972 grey painting by Gerhard Richter and screwed table legs under it in order to make it look like a table. A piece, rather valuable at the time, purposefully devaluated by transforming it into a somehow reverse ready-made. The process is similar to what Mollino did: a form of appropriation of an existing work in order to create a new context.

Political Facade I

In our 2009-competition entry for the German embassy in Belgrade, we were confronted with the problem of architecture as a political display. The call by the German Foreign Ministry asked for a new building on a prominent site which today is occupied by a remarkable building: an existing structure from the early 1970s which is a political landmark. It is a late modernist Yugoslav building, highly symbolic for the beginning of the *Entspannungspolitik* which Willy Brandt initiated at that time, following ten years of cold war, by reopening the West-German embassies in all socialist countries. Even so, the building today is supposed to be demolished. Our design turns the logic of erasure around, proposing the demolition of the technically exhausted building but not of its remarkable structural concrete facade. By designing a white cube behind the existing facade we produce a new context that at once highlights and alienates the historical fragment. It is a transfer of the museum condition into the city in which a familiar object is being transformed into an object on display. The fact that the political representatives in the jury vetoed our design gave a demonstration of the political nature of our proposed architectural move and uncovered the suppressed political nature of the allegedly technical demolition.

Political Facade II

Humboldt Forum, the reconstruction of the historical castle in Berlin, 2008. A strange competition as the organisers already had a plan for the reconstruction of the facades; no suggestions were required for this

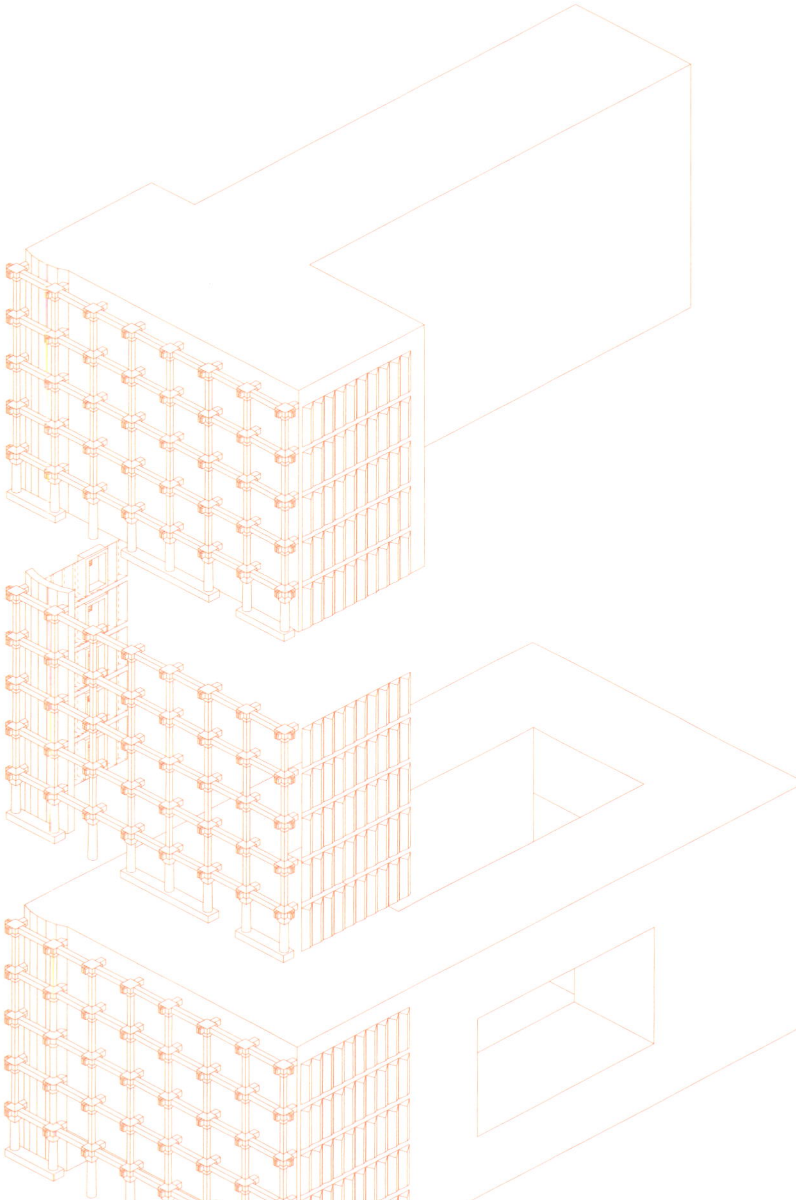

German Embassy Belgrade,
competition entry, 2009.

Reconstruction of the Berlin Castle, competition entry, 2008.

particular part of the project. The Berlin castle had been demolished in the 1950s by the socialist government and of course it is a political issue to decide to rebuild the castle. Our point was that you cannot rebuild a castle which has been absent for half a century as if it were a work of ordinary city repair. Rather it means initiating an experiment of conscious architectural reproduction, being aware that the issue of reproduction itself today has achieved a major role in all parts of our society. We proposed a model of the historical castle, 1:1 scale. As full volumetric model of the historical event, it will interact with the surrounding structures, above all Schinkel's Altes Museum. It will be able to engage Schinkel in his yet to be realised plan for an active relation between Museum and castle by opening the new facade instead of reconstructing the historical fortress-like terraces on this side. A massive two meter thick brick wall will give form to the huge architectural model and appear in the urban space as a relief without decoration. In the event of successful fundraising by private initiatives in favour of historical reconstruction, stone ornaments and stuccos will be applied in a second building phase, thus putting the reproduction process itself on display. The project obtained a special mention but did not win due to vetoes by the political representatives, as again the display of a historical facade revealed itself to be the political point of conflict.

Use

Komuna Fundamento is our 1:1 contribution for the Venice Architecture Biennale 2012. Curator David Chipperfield's motto *Common Ground* meant for us that you aim at disappearing in the exhibition, entering the exhibition space and, somehow, mingling. We realised a big bench made of grey brick, a pediment in front of the Palazzo delle Esposizioni blocking the usual way into it. The construction incorporates a tree that was already there. Many visitors did not even recognise the construction as part of the exhibition. In fact we asked not to put any label on or next to this object. The intervention became architecture just because people sat on and started using it. We think of physical use as a real 1:1 experience that

Reconstruction of the Berlin Castle, competition entry, 2008.

Komuna Fundamento, installation view, Venice Architecture Biennale 2012.

nale

Komuna Fundamento, installation view, Venice Architecture Biennale 2012.

distinguishes architecture from most other arts. Inside the Palazzo delle Esposizioni we realised another object as the counter-image or counter-space of the first one. The space outside of the Palazzo delle Esposizioni is a big sculptural intervention creating space around it, while the space inside is a place you can move through, a hollow intervention creating space within, used to exhibit photography by Candida Höfer and Armin Linke, two photographers we have worked with for many years, who share our interest in the relational presence of space.

Curatorial Design

Making the exhibition *Carlo Mollino. Maniera Moderna* at the Haus der Kunst in Munich in 2011, I asked myself what it means to make a monographic exhibition.
The architect Carlo Mollino is quite recognised in both the art and design worlds but paradoxically largely ignored in architectural history. This was a good starting point for us and it was important to exhibit Mollino in an art museum. We wanted to create a real experience as I do not agree that architecture cannot be exhibited as a one-to-one experience in an exhibition. Architecture is not only about building or about space making but also about the narration and perception of reality.
Carlo Mollino is an architect who uses many conceptual tools. This is what we decided to show. Of course that is still not enough to render an experience, so a further step was to ask Armin Linke to co-curate the exhibition and to be engaged in the show as an artist. I think that this decision was important in terms of curatorial design because it dealt with the issue of what it means to make a concept interact with direct authorship. Armin Linke travelled all the Mollino places and made large format, colour photographs of the buildings and spaces as he found them, more often than not abandoned or untidy. This was a way for us to take a new look and open new perspectives on the work of Mollino, allowing the visitor to reach a closeness to the work of the architect and make an experience in the exhibition. I would argue that, although these photographs are not life size, the perceptive experience that they deliver is 1:1 as it is not at all illustrative.

Carlo Mollino. Maniera Moderna, installation view with Mollino's antifascism monument photographed by Armin Linke, Haus der Kunst, Munich, 2011.

Carlo Mollino. Maniera Moderna, installation view with furniture treated as sculptures on high pedestals, Haus der Kunst, Munich, 2011.

Let me take as an example a picture by Linke of Mollino's antifascism monument. When he went there, he happened to assist and photograph the ritual meeting of the partisans' relatives and followers who regularly meet there to commemorate. The antifascist monument is not represented as a piece of sculpture but as something that is being used, in a political way, for the commemoration of the partisans. The picture witnesses an active use of Mollino's structure and I would say that this is very important for an exhibition, because it actually shows the kind of update it is able to produce.
We had a limited number of furniture pieces by Carlo Mollino on exhibit. We constructed a sort of a theatre for these objects putting them on high pedestals and fully treating them as sculptures. The objects lost their closeness to the earth where they are expected to be used and we went a step further and transformed them into objects that you almost look at on eye level – in this way these objects become theatrical and architectural and this is another way of making a 1:1 experience. Since you cannot sit on or touch and use them, you have to create another and even alienated way of translating 1:1.
Then we had one room of projections, where we used Mollino's photography of his interiors. Next to the original framed vintage prints exhibited on the wall we projected a number of photographs on three large walls, giving the visitor the freedom to move into these interiors. The pictures changed in a slideshow and the visitor could move in these historical environments seen through the eyes of Carlo Mollino. This is a way of having a 1:1 experience using Mollino's photographs.
In the exhibition we had a sculptural wood-part of a table that we exhibited without the glass surface in order to move one step further in showing it as a sculpture; not only did we take off the glass top but we also placed it on a pedestal so that the object became something like an historical structure, a skeleton. You could see on the wall behind this object the original documentation including the technical drawings as we generated a relation between the work (how you draw and make the table) and the piece itself.
We showed a film made by Armin Linke about how peo-

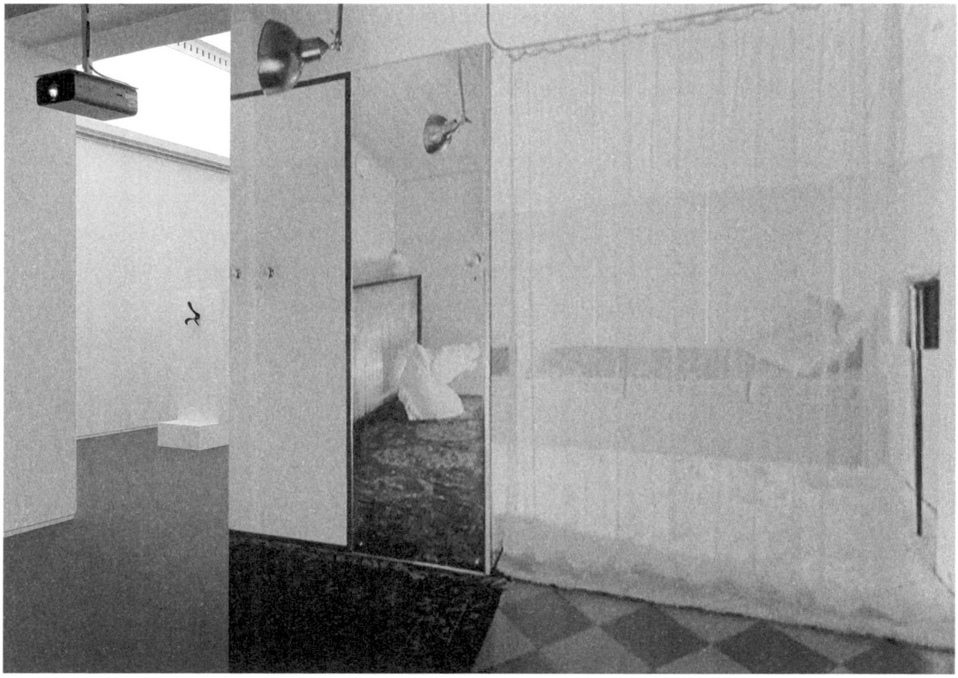

Carlo Mollino. Maniera Moderna, **installation view with with room of projections as 1:1 experience, Haus der Kunst, Munich, 2011.**

ple live with Mollino's artefacts. There is a last villa left that is fully furnished and completely designed by Mollino and the owners are still using it as a holiday home. In Linke's video you see how they move the table through the garden. The video shows a gentle and unspectacular way of living within the spaces designed by Mollino and with Mollino himself. You can look at this film and almost feel that you are invited to lunch in this house. In different ways we added a series of layers of reality to the show as we did not see it as a form of documentation but as a form of direct experience.

7 ROOMS, 21 PERSPECTIVES
curated by *OFFICE Kersten Geers*
David Van Severen and Bas Princen

GARDEN PAVILION
VENICE ARCHITECTURE BIENNALE
29 AUGUST–21 NOVEMBER 2011

7 Rooms, 21 Perspectives, view of the porch.

7 Rooms, 21 Perspectives,
installation view.

7 Rooms, 21 Perspectives,
installation view with *Grid II*
by Bas Princen.

7 Rooms, 21 Perspectives, installation view with *Pavilion (Venice)* by Bas Princen.

7 Rooms, 21 Perspectives, installation view with *Ring Road (Findeq/Cevta)* by Bas Princen (left) and *Cité Refuge* by OFFICE Kersten Geers David Van Severen (right).

7 Rooms, 21 Perspectives, installation view with *A Grammar for the City* by OFFICE Kersten Geers David Van Severen (left) and *Botanic Garden (Xiamen)* by Bas Princen (right).

interview by *Eva Mair*
recorded in Brussels
in May 2014

7 ROOMS, 21 PERSPECTIVES

This conversation should analyse your exhibition named *7 rooms, 21 perspectives* which you presented together with Bas Princen at the Garden Pavilion during the 2010 Architecture Biennale in Venice. The show worked upon different layers – the pictures and collages on steel plates interacted with the spatial interventions on the hitherto disused ammunition warehouse. The elements seemed to dialogue with and reference each other. What was the task and how did you approach the commission?

The whole thing of the Biennale was rather a strange story. I think the one who was instrumental in that logic was Moritz Küng, with whom we had already worked before and who had worked with Sanaa as well.[1]
When we were invited we were brought to the very end of the Arsenale-area. Piet Oudolf was commissioned to work on the garden and it seems that during his transformation of the savaged green area into a proper garden, they sort of discovered a building. The building was obviously always there but I think it was never really on the radar as being a place that belonged to the Architecture Biennale. Apparently, it had been used a couple of years earlier for some video installations during an Art Biennale. It was pretty peculiar and Kazuyo Sejima suddenly decided that we should exhibit in this space. They offered us a budget which was close to nothing, plus there was almost no time left and we were left with this bizarre building completely overgrown with plants.

1 Moritz Küng curated the exhibition *Kazuyo Sejima + Ryue Nishizawa / SANAA & Walter Niedermayr* at deSingel International Art Campus in Antwerp, 15 February–6 May 2007, as the show *OFFICE Kersten Geers and David Van Severen 7 Rooms*, in the same location as well as the show , 5 March–3 May 2009.

So it was confusing at first.

We are quite convinced that it is not possible to invent anything new in architecture – as well as in cultural work in general for that matter. You're always reworking and re-appropriating things and moving on from somewhere – consciously or unconsciously. The building happened to be a building with seven rooms. And the show we did the year before at deSingel was a seven-room show.

Of course we did not want to do the very same show. That would not be possible. In fact the show at the Garden Pavilion – consisting of pictures of Bas Princen and our collages – is actually an emulation of a circumstance, it's a re-enactment or a kind of reworking of that same *7 Rooms* exhibition in the deSingel. The decision to simply do the same show, but with other means, and to re-use all the decisions we had already taken as starting points, all of a sudden gave us a track. In the deSingel we turned the hallway into an enfilade by simply inserting eight walls. The eight walls would make the seven rooms, which allowed us to form families of objects: there were mainly objects on tables, here and there a collage, and pictures of Bas Princen on the wall.

So the catalogue of the *7 Rooms* exhibition in Antwerp is in a way the *secret guide* to the Garden Pavilion in Venice, which then was almost like the afterthought, contemplating the idea of the same show but in secrecy. It was by stumbling upon this that we realized that actually there was something else to talk about and this was the relationship between the pictures of Bas and our perspectival drawings or collages. In the second room for example – the Villa Room – suddenly a picture of Bas Princen, which wasn't shown at the deSingel, dialogued with a perspective of the so called Villa Voka[2], which is actually not a villa, making it seem as if it has always been related to it in some way. I knew the picture very well. So it was almost as if we had made the Villa Voka with the picture of Bas in the back.

2 *Villa Voka*, Chamber of Commerce, Kortrijk, BE, 2008–2010

7 Rooms, installation view,
deSingel, Antwerp, 2009.

Wall Pavilion, installation view, Shenzen Bi-City Biennial of Urbanism and Architecture 2013–2014.

So your first decision then, taken together with Bas Princen, was to start from the *7 Rooms* exhibition and show your mutual approach and interest towards the image and the perspectival depiction. Can you explain the process that led from those thoughts to the spatial intervention and the exhibition setting as a whole?

We needed to organise the exhibition in the quickest possible way and with the *7 Rooms* we had a guide.
We did not want to make a monographic show. We did not want to show architecture – in the deSingle we had shown architecture models, but because of the limited budget we could not transport them to Venice. We did not want to show prints on paper because in that space with a terrible climate they would not have survived two months. And in the end there was the challenge to make a Biennale contribution two years after *After the Party*[3], where we had declared that it made no sense anymore to document architecture and show representations of architecture. So it was impossible to then just show models. That made no sense. Our question was: "What after this?".
In fact, from the very beginning we wanted to avoid doing another 1:1 intervention because we had already done it. We thought that for us it had been successful: the wall, the empty pavilion, the confetti – that was the thing we wanted to say.
In a certain way we wanted to make a classic exhibition. We wanted to emphasize something we hadn't emphasized enough before, which was the collaboration with Bas. We felt it was the right moment to touch upon another thing, which is fundamental for us: the perspective – our constructed perspectives, the framing and the cutting: all things which Bas does in his pictures too – and how close we felt to his work. All our work is full of these multiple layers. It was showing to people fragments of a train of thought, which had always been there, but

3 *After the Party,* **OFFICE Kersten Geers David Van Severen, Belgian contribution at the 11th Venice Architecture Biennale, 14 September–23 November 2008.**

never shown. We are good friends of Bas. We know most of his pictures from early on. So they were there, they were part of our thinking anyhow and I guess we wanted to show that.

Furthermore, we wanted to contemplate how you could show this relationship in that particular space. The steel plates allowed us to print on a material that would not deteriorate. We decided to put our work in relation to that of Bas. Our perspectives are always smaller than his pictures. The steel plates required us to clean the rooms. Although we then painted all the doors white, we realized that it was not enough. We needed a kind of porch. So we added a piece of architecture, which allowed us to do exactly what we did in the deSingel, and by doing that we mediated the garden and the building. So even before you are aware of it, again you make a 1:1 intervention. It's the parable of cultural production in general – the exact thing you want to avoid but which, in the end you don't avoid at all.

We are result-minded. We don't like to show the process. We like process a lot, but we don't show it. Nowhere. These are the things you can see from us. I can explain if you ask, but I'll never show you because we think that the power of architecture production, perhaps of cultural production in general, also of the *mise en scéne* of an exhibition, is that at a certain point you decide: "This is the result" and it shows itself in all its ambiguity.

In your text *Words without thoughts never to heaven go*[4] you say that architecture is about making artefacts. You don't make a difference between different manifestations of architecture, be they drawings, models or buildings. Your curatorial challenge in an exhibition is then how to combine, to transform and to point out the particular thought you have in mind. What was important for you in this set or combination of artefacts?

4 OFFICE Kersten Geers David Van Severen, Words without thoughts never to heaven go, *2G nr. 63*, Gustavo Gili, Barcelona 2012, pp. 162-166

When we – David, Bas, I and some collaborators from the office – in August installed the exhibition ourselves, Bas took this picture. It's not a collage, it's a picture![5] Many people continue to think that this is not a picture, but a collage. We decided on the spot to put this picture outside, against the wall, which somehow mimics the picture and you get a very strange inner rhyme. The whole thing starts to iterate. Everything densifies to such a point that it is no longer clear to anyone what was first, what is why, and what is where. The installation as a whole talks about Bas and us, about perspective, about the status of architecture, about the difference between – I would say – building and architecture. Not that architecture is more beautiful than building, but that there are intensions behind architecture: the idea of measuring and numerous references that are important; yet we believe there's no need to point these things out. In a strange way you can also understand this as a kind of remake of the Belgian Pavilion. Adding the gravel was in a way a gesture not unlike adding the confetti. It was very similar actually. And although it doesn't look like it, in the end it was the same act. The Belgian Pavilion was very direct – black and white, in and out. The Garden Pavilion is ambiguous, but the result is quite the same. We added the columns and the porch and appropriated that part of the garden as part of the building in very much the same way we did at the Belgian Pavilion. We even took the same chairs, but we painted them white. In the Belgian Pavilion we painted the very light aluminium chairs grey because we wanted them to look like the chairs of the Jardin du Luxembourg, which are typically just brown-grey. But in the Garden Pavilion we painted everything white since we were dealing both with the selected pictures and the old ammunition storehouse by considering the questions: "What is architecture? What do you need to add so that the building becomes architecture?". Everything which was added – the doors, the columns the chairs – was white. But at the same time the chair obviously carried with it an echo of that previous chair, because it's the same.

5 See the picture at page 93.

Is the exhibition a context where you experiment, in a more indepencent way, your beliefs, with references and with collaborations as, for example, that with Bas Princen? How did this or other exhibitions contribute to the development of your practice?

First of all working with Bas is very specific. Recently we did another Pavilion with him in Shenzhen[6]. This circular pavilion is in a way like panorama pavilions – those buildings that used to be made about 150 years ago. You enter them and you somehow have the idea that you are looking over a certain scene. It has a lot to do with an experiment which examines questions like: "What's the status of the image, the status of the building, the building as an image?". It relates to our idea of the three-dimensional, of the two-dimensional and of the landscape we originated. There's also a contemplation of form, structure and construction. The very thin brick wall is only standing because it's laid out in a circular form. That's a certain line of experimentation but it's very specific because it's the result of a collaboration.
The Garden Pavilion started as a way of selecting perspectives and then, while doing that, it moved. It's not that David and I made the architecture for the content, we came up with the spatial element altogether.
An exhibition allows you to push an idea because it always has to be done in the shortest possible time and not many people ask too many questions. The two shows we did in the Bozar here in Brussels, *The world of Lucas Cranach*[7] and *Indomania*[8], are almost mock-up architecture dealing with issues like: "What's the idea of sequence? What's the idea of enfilade? How do you frame things?". For example, the Cranach show was very much a sequence of spaces. We tried to contemplate the architecture of Victor Horta, the architect of the building.

6 ***Wall Pavilion,*** **Shenzen Bi-City Biennial of Urbanism and Architecture, 06 December 2013–28 February 2014.**
7 ***The world of Lucas Cranach,*** **Bozar Centre for Fine Arts, Brussels, 20 October 2010–23 January 2011.**
8 ***Indomania,*** **Bozar Centre for Fine Arts, Brussels, 16 OCtober 2013–26 January 2014.**

Since we worked on the walls for that exhibition, for the India show we decided to concentrate on the ceiling and on the floor.

Maybe it's just a quicker way to produce an output – to materialise ideas you have in mind...

Yes, you can do crazy tests on materialization or try things about which we are not yet sure. This is really good. Can you make something out of laminate rather than out of real marble? Is it ok? In an exhibition you can try that. It doesn't harm anybody and they might not even see it.
No project really has a specific status. For example, the three Oasis Pavilions were meant as temporary buildings and initially seemed to be relatively quickly made. However, their construction ended up not being so quick; they took longer to build than expected and then they remained as permanent structures. So they became in a strange way architecture. In the involvement with the pavilions we worked on privacy, on the green, on correcting a found situation and on the screen-like skin of the building – things that had been developed in parallel with other projects. And so yes, an exhibition looks like something quickly devised and realised, but often it is not. Compared to a building, it's obviously something that requires less of a budget. It allows you to test.

I would like to come back to the 1:1 intervention. Many other contributors to the 2010 Biennale intervened in their given space and created empirical situations, 1:1 experiences of architecture for the audience. Do you see in this approach within the exhibition-practices an emerging possibility to discuss and mediate architecture?

Yes, it's true. I think that in terms of context, this was important. A secret *souffleur* in the Biennale might have been Moritz Küng. I think he was at that time quite close to Kazuyo Sejima and Yuko Hasegawa and insisting in this idea of 1:1 as a possibility for exhibiting architecture. Moritz Küng's approach towards exposing architecture is that you cannot really expose it. In the Belgian Pavilion at the 2008 Biennale he forced the competitors to make a 1:1 intervention. We proposed this wall, which was probably the most radical of the submitted projects, but nevertheless all of the others were also 1:1. And I have the feeling that the idea of working with as few contributors as possible might have been his because of his obsession with reduction.

We were invited late in the process of the 2010 Biennale and they were already able to explain to us what everybody was doing and we thought let's not do 1:1, let's introduce perspective. They were somehow happy that we did accept that strange place in the back, next to that beautiful garden. Whatever we would have done, would have been ok. It is even true that when we then presented what we wanted to do, we did not just show them the pictures and perspectives but also the roof, so there was never really a doubt. Maybe they liked the roof after all.

I really do not think that you only have to make installations to do or to show architecture. I often had that discussion at that time and I still have it with Moritz Küng. I think, yes, great, but only when it makes sense. And we have to be careful. People are very simplistic. With every new fashion – whether it be journalism or let's say now 1:1 – you mostly have only a few good projects.

Do you think this 1:1 comes along with a specific way of thinking on architecture that pertains to the generation of architects you belong to?

It's increasingly harder to understand what our generation thinks. I don't know. I think we are very much part of a movement against the diagram, diagrammatic thinking about architecture. There was a certain idea of architecture originating in Holland, but not only there,

in the late 90s and early 2000s, which thought that architecture could solve things. It's very simple: you have a problem and you resolve it through a diagram. The diagram can be materialised and that's the architecture. The argument against this approach is complex. I wouldn't say that that's an argument in favour of a 1:1 approach *per se*. It's just an argument for architecture being architecture, being itself and not something else. In other words, trying to reconnect to principles of architecture, trying to reconnect to the tools of architecture, to understanding that a wall is a wall, that architecture doesn't resolve anything, but is rather an obstruction, a problem (and a rather interesting problem at that) and that we do not have to sell people things, which we are incapable of doing anyway. I think that's very much an area to which we belong.
And then there is a phenomenological aspect related to our work, which seems to be inspired by something entirely different: our fascination with Los Angeles. We have a kind of very European part of us, but then there is another part looking at L.A.. This has been fundamental to me and to David from the very beginning. Already in our diploma projects we had an obsession with Hockney and L.A., which of course comes back in our idea of presentation. Through Hockney came Piero della Francesca, and through Piero della Francesca the Renaissance, and through the Renaissance Bramante, and through Bramante the idea of defining space in a painterly way.
So there has always been this ambiguity in our work. There's all this and I suppose there's 1:1, but always in an ambiguous form.

The Garden Pavilion is not the only experience you had with such large events like the Biennale. This kind of event seems to be becoming more and more popular around the world: however, along with this boom there is less and less time for conducting specific research and hence deciding what and how to exhibit. As you described your way of working, you always follow your own investigations. What does it mean for you – in the role of an invited contributor – to be part of such events? Do you consider the topic or just make your own next step?

Indeed we never join anything. We just do our own work. And of course when you present it you might be influenced by the questions they ask. They give you a space. So something happens with that space. But there's another reason why we do things. We just don't talk about it. The topic of the Bi-City Biennale of Urbanism/Architecture in Shenzhen was *Urban Borders* and they immediately thought of our border crossing project[9].

I remember I called Bas and suggested doing another step in our experiment on the perspective. So we presented the pavilion and they were a bit surprised at first. But we said that that's what we want to do and then somehow they accepted it.

I'm highly sceptical about this so-called pseudo-research for the sake of the event. I mean, we do research in a way – there's a formal research you develop – but that has nothing to do with what people commonly consider research. Then maybe we find more than they find. Sometimes we see an invitation for an exhibition as a great opportunity for something and sometimes maybe also not. But it's always the same dilemma you have with any assignment.

In all these exhibitions we did touch upon many things and there indeed I think you were right with your question before about an experimentation that contributes to the developing of our practice. We designed a show in the *MOMU,* the Fashion Museum in Antwerp,[10] only with railings and prints on the floor. There was nothing else. We are experimenting with these projects where in a way we try to make spaces with no walls. The *Solo House*[11] is quite an extreme example of that. There are only columns. After making many houses with only

9 *Border Garden,* international competition (1st prize), 2005.

10 *Living Fashion. Women's Daily Wear 1750–1950,* Mode Museum, Momu, Antwerp, 21 March–12 August 2012.

11 *Solo,* villa near Barcelona, under development, 2012-

walls, now there's only distance and the way to mediate this distance. There are many of these connections.

Also the *Solo chair*[12] is connected to that – in another way...

Yes, the *Solo chair* derived in a way from the plan of the *Solo* House. It's a cloud of things. And that's also how we deal with exhibition questions.

12 *Solo chair,* limited edition furniture for MANIERA, Brussels, 2014.

The World of Lucas Cranach, installation view, Bozar Centre for Fine Arts, Brussels, 2010–2011.

Indomania, installation view, Bozar Centre for Fine Arts, Brussels, 2013–2014.

Pearl Route collage, 2012.

Oasis, Sharyah Art Biennial,
2012–2013.

Solo chair, limited edition furniture for MANIERA, Brussels, 2014.

ON THE SIDE OF THE PUBLIC

For a long time the architecture exhibition has been considered as an event that almost exclusively addresses a public of experts. This is a significant matter if we assume everyone makes a daily experience of architecture and of the built realm. This issue becomes the reason for shifting the attention away from the places where the object of this study occurs and toward the public's consumption of the architecture exhibition as well as toward the relationship between the devices introduced in the show and their reception on part of the visitors. A first level worth examining is, obviously, the persuasive power of the exhibition maker on the viewer in defining an opinion about the exhibition content.
A second level relates to the fact that media and devices often generate a gap, or distance, between content and recipient. Drawings (and often even photographs) represent ideal conditions conceived by a designer in a phase that precedes the realisation; three-dimensional models enter into relationship with the visitor and try to engage him or her with the issues at hand.
In general, however, we feel external to the world represented by the model, we literally feel left out, while the experience of inhabiting architecture is most certainly connected with the possibility of entering and being part of it. It is in this context that the contributions presented here deal with issues related to the necessity of investigating the possible forms and strategies of communication that might be included in the exhibitions (e.g. narrations, dialogues, discourses) as essential parts of the exhibition system.
With her contribution Emanuela De Cecco directs a sharp eye to the necessary negotiations between exhibition maker and visitor, focussing on the different

forms of the exhibition space and on how these can influence the space of the narration, the narration itself and the relationship with the public. The text works on the different (also invisible) interaction levels between the actors, using instruments borrowed from semiotic and communication studies. The author recognises the importance of allowing the viewer autonomy in the visit and of allowing some of the aspects to remain unexplained so as to avoid the risk of having everything clarified and of erasing all degrees of freedom.

She describes an architecture model inserted in the Istanbul Biennale in 2011 (the model of the exhibition space itself) which caused distress to the whole system: was it meant as signage or was it an object that acquired a peculiar *aura* due to its displacement?

The author – responsible for the setting of the exhibition – is Ryue Nishizawa, who was involved in the Venice Architecture Biennale *People Meet in Architecture* one year earlier, and his assignment is certainly aimed at elevating the value of the exhibition. Furthermore, the fact that next to the examined model there is a caption with *directions for use printed on it,* contributes to reducing the visitor's degree of freedom. The voices of the different people involved in the production of an exhibition could instead generate a sort of symphony, as described in the detailed reference to the exhibition *Geschichten im Konflikt* at the Haus der Kunst in Munich.

Something Fantastic have recently been involved as set designers in the production of shows. Their work is about different exhibition typologies in which the display changes according to the public: from the setting of a workshop with the inhabitants of a neighbourhood

in Rio de Janeiro to the installation of works in an art exhibition. The architects focus their attention on the dialogue between the two- and three-dimensional spaces projected into the space of the show, as it happens not only for the graphic grid in the exhibition space of *Raumproduktion* at the Kunsthalle Düsseldorf, but also for the posters for the final exhibition of the project *Cidade de Deus,* which are essential to the exhibition and invite the neighbourhood inhabitants to activate the workshop spaces.
Ilka and Andreas Ruby, who consider architecture the most public of all arts because it is always around us, focus on the sense of respect that many feel towards this discipline, and on the fact that the discourse about architecture can be very elitist and interdictive to a broad public. Their approach arises from the perception of architecture as a place of social interaction translated in the language of their exhibitions. In their contribution Ilka and Andreas Ruby refer to possible allusions that they put to use on various occasions, occasions in which they experiment with forms of public participation in the exhibition and which culminate with the Druot, Lacaton and Vassal exhibition at the DAM (Deutsches Architekturmuseum) in Frankfurt. The two curators concentrate on the reception of the viewer and maintain their position, certain that the architecture practice and architectural discourse should not drift apart. The exhibition is an intervention in real scale. In this immersive show we are asked to experience the exhibited space by inhabiting an image.
The photographic representation bursts conspicuously into the show not as a tool to represent absent archi-

tecture but as a means of creating the exhibition space by way of transforming it.
Andres Lepik shares a similar attitude and places as central to his contribution the choice of issues to be dealt with within the architecture exhibition and the moment of reception by the public. The approach is directed by a will to get close to as wide a public as possible, both in regards to the content as well as the display forms. In the projects presented, which range from his very first experiences as a curator to his work for MoMA, Andres Lepik, presently director of the Architecture Museum of the TU München, gently approaches visitors instead of overwhelming them.

THE EXHIBITION SPACE AS REPRESENTATION OF IDEOLOGY AND STORIES

Emanuela De Cecco

Starting from a general consideration on the leading dynamics that regulate the run of the present art system, this contribution takes into consideration two different ways of relating to the space put to use by two recent contemporary art exhibitions: the 12th Istanbul Biennale (2011) and Geschichten im Konflikt (2012) at the Haus der Kunst in Munich. In the first case the question develops from analysing the way in which the exhibition is displayed. In the second case the spatial issue concentrates on the presence of a series of photographs, shot by Hans Haacke – at that time student of the Kassel Academy of Art – during Documenta 2 (1955). The photographs reflect the artist's interest in the life that develops in the exhibition space due to the presence of visitors as well as in the main works exhibited which, by the way, marked the European celebration of American Abstract Expressionism that established itself in those years as an emblematic movement of modernity. In both cases the space is considered as the fundamental element contributing to the ideological makeup of the two exhibitions.

In a 2012 article published in December on *Artforum*, the well-known art historian Benjamin Buchloh, who has written important essays on 20th century artists and movements, built a fierce diagnosis of the contemporary art world and its dynamics.
I will start from the first part of that work, focusing the attention on some passages that seem to be of the uttermost importance to me. The author bases his thoughts on a temporal arch (from 1860 to the beginning of the 1970s) in which "artists, who shared an avant-garde culture, have created models of alternative social relations, languages and spaces of distinction, concepts of critique and counter memory" (ibid.), that is, during that period when the artistic action was indeed the result of the artists' choice to take explicitly unconventional and utopian positions, aimed at opposing the dominant ideology and forms of power through which such ideology manifested itself. According to Buchloh, the ultimate resistance

should be traced back to the moment when forms of advanced capitalism began to strategically assimilate, instead of directly face, conflicting phenomena, with the result of eliminating their bursting effects. That was the time when artists understood how museums were participating in the imposition of forms of control through the process of canonization, showing a sort of tolerance after having kept it isolated inside their structures for a long time. After this new awareness, artists gave birth to the so called *institutional critique* (Asher, Buren, Haacke), even if in those same years (1975) Warhol was positively stating the indissoluble relation between art and business in *The Philosophy of Andy Warhol.*

Buchloh recognises that Warhol prophesied, in what he considered to be a parody, "the total permeation of the cultural sphere by the economic operations of finance capital and its attendant ethos and social structures" that since the 80s has provoked structural changes in the sphere of production and in artistic acceptance, reflecting also on key places like museums, universities, and libraries (ibid.) in the United States and other western countries.

Without focusing on the museum, Bourdieu talks about the economics of symbolic goods (1984), Pine-Gilmore on the economics of experiences (1999), and Rifkin describes the processes of value which systematically proceed the transformation of the collective fields of culture into commodified experiences (2000) and again, Rem Koolhaas writes that "museums are giving up to shopping in order to survive" (2002).

Concentrating on the museum of contemporary art, Rosalind Krauss underlines in *The Cultural Logic of the Late Capitalistic Museum* (1990) the pervasiveness of market logic in the cultural sphere and, consequently, the transformation of the museum into a factory of entertainment and leisure time. More recently, Hal Foster (*The Art-Architecture Complex,* 2011), recalling precedent issues, traces the parallel paths of art and architecture anticipating the turning point between the 50s and the 60s when "the consumerist superficiality of signs and [the] seriality of objects affected architecture and urbanism as well as painting and sculpture" (Foster, ibid.). Starting from different experiences and points of view, these authors, along with many others, agreed on the transformation of the cultural institution, including museums of contemporary art, from *special* protected places into common places governed by the same rules. The link between mass entertainment and museums is a direct consequence of this transformation. And even if we could trace the origin of this phenomenon back in time, as many of the authors cited above did, I do not wish to shift the attention from the present time.

We can certainly assert that, starting from the 80s, this phenomenon experienced an acceleration and expansion also in geographical terms, involving such countries as China, India, and Brazil, which were not present in the art world as it was characterised in the 20th century. Overall, more than a shift in paradigm, the transformation involves a change in quantity (of new museums, art exhibitions, of record prices established in art auctions), resulting in the consolidation of certain judging criteria for art: first of all by measuring success by economic terms and visibility (the number of spectators) – indexes which do not pertain only to the art world – and, at the same time, in the weakening of the items which do not consider this scenery as a unique model.

In the Empire's provinces (including Italy) it often happens that many art exhibitions are announced with overwhelming tones, with a mixture of outdated terms like *masterpiece, uniqueness, beauty* and new ones like *atmosphere* and *intensity,* where a reference to the type of experience Jameson called "hysterical sublime" can be noted (Jameson, 1984).

Concerning *beauty,* a concept which was dramatically excluded from the distinctive art criteria of the 20th century, Fulvio Carmagnola redefined it in the contemporary post-industrial economy as "a developing requirement, which *does* something, something very concrete, it does the value of the product, what allows it to play its role in the field of communication" (Carmagnola, 2009).

Yet the concise coordinates drawn thus far do give a reliable picture of the state of art today; nevertheless, a consideration on how the exhibition space is designed and what role the spectator plays should start from those coordinates using different analytical instruments than those belonging to the art discourse. A recent reinterpretation of Michael Baxandall's essay enforces this position. In *Exhibiting Intention: Some Preconditions of the Visual Display of Culturally Purposeful Objects* (1991), he considers a *certain kind of exhibition* – a traditional exhibition of historical-anthropological artefacts of a museum collection where objects are exhibited inside specific boxes or hung on the walls, together with descriptive labels and a catalogue – and a *certain type of spectator* – an adult member of a developed society who holds an idea of museum, and understands the museum as heritage, a learning tool. Extremely synthesised, the core concept of this text consists of a redefinition of the exhibition space as a field where three independent elements with different orientations interact: those which produce objects, those which show them, and those which watch them.

The text also highlights the curator's necessity of thinking of the spectator as an active subject and, consequently, that his work consists in creating the necessary conditions to allow for the space shared by those three elements to exist, as well as in guaranteeing that the encounter between the spectator and the art work is conditioned as little as possible.

The importance of these statements lies in the fact that they suggest an approach that protects the freedom of choosing how to interact with all that is shown in an exhibition, that is, an approach which is distant from the one which is only concerned with not abandoning the spectator to himself, with letting museums overload exhibitions with didactic apparatus so that nothing remains unexplained.

Though I consider this a fundamental point to Baxandall's argument, upon rereading it after quite some time, I was led to interpret an aspect of it differently than I had at first, an aspect which now seems to stand out more clearly than when it was written.

Paradoxically, what struck me the most was the fact that all the considerations the author made refer to the cultural field (museum life was conceived exclusively as a knowledge experience), but there are no indications on how the analysed subjects (art works, labels, spectators)

Setting of the 12th Istanbul Biennial, model view, 2011.

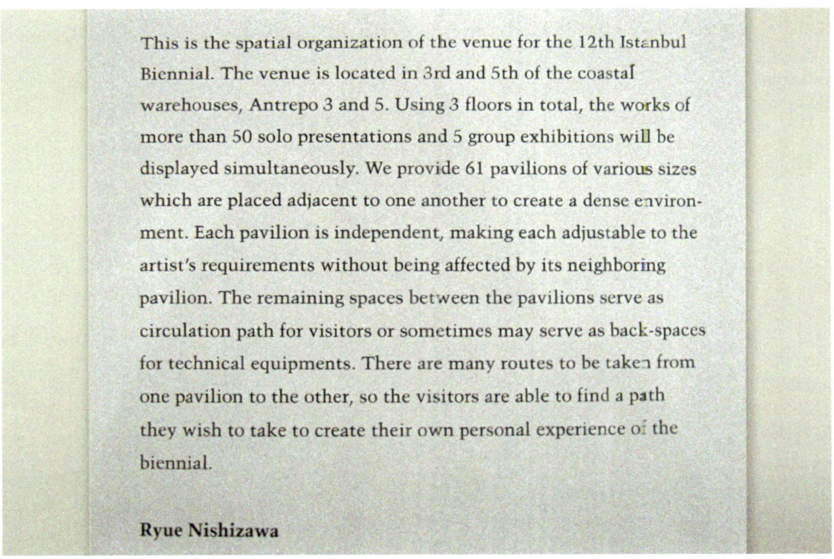

Caption for the model of the setting of the 12th Istanbul Biennial, 2011.

have been structurally modified by the transformation of the museum and thus by the change which has occurred to the place where they encounter one another.
This is more evident in temporary exhibitions, but we can also spot the influence of this change in permanent collections, which are, in many cases, less permanent than before (as it is for the Tate Modern in London, the Museum of Modern Art in Frankfurt, the Triennale Design Museum in Milan, where collections are periodically set up). The same could be said when analysing the exhibition space in such a way that the discourse focuses only on those elements which concretely define the disposition of art works, or the paths followed by the spectator, and exclude the frame within which the exhibition is shaped. These aspects are, and remain, central elements but they should not be considered the *only* reference by those who design them (curators and designers) or by those who experience them (the public); rather they should be envisioned by both actors quoted above from not just a functional viewpoint, but from a symbolic and communicational point of view as well.
In this regards I find it useful to recall the example of the Istanbul Biennale of 2011 (curated by Jean Hoffman and Adrian Pedrosa) which witnessed for the first time a model of the actual exhibition being displayed within the exhibition space itself. The model was realised by Ryue Nishizawa of Sejima and Nishizawa and Associates (SANAA), Tokyo, and was considered an innovative piece in an art exhibition, in particular the caption describing the model. It is an analytic/descriptive explanation, with hints at the functional aspects (following Roman Jakobson's theory about language's function), which ends with a description of the movement modalities thought for the spectators, where accent is put on their/our independence in deciding how to visit the exhibition: "to create their own personal experience of the biennale".
As a spectator myself of that Biennale exhibition, I experienced a great sense of constraint in witnessing the space, as has rarely happened to me on prior occasions.
At the end of the itinerary, after a few hours spent in a hive of 61 pavilions, I was surprised to read that the exhibition grounds had been conceived as an invitation

to freely manage our own movement, especially because I had experienced it as an exercise of strong control directed to us.
The exhibition was based on a reinterpretation of the work by Felix Gonzalez-Torres. Curators spotted some thematic categories constituting the generating theme of an independent exhibition, one in which public communication (in the form of posters adapted from famous works by the same artist but with different messages) could have internal coherence if the invitation to manage the itinerary in an autonomous way also included that this autonomy was contained in a well-defined grid, both from a thematic point of view (the choice of considering the artist's work as the unique engine of the exhibition and the choice of categorising its work, an always delicate operation), and from a spatial point of view (the choice of giving such a definite set to the staging which was set free in all the preceding editions of the biennale hosted in the same place, with some exception thought in relation with the presence of a considerable number of video shows which demand for dim areas).
What might seem a negligible detail appears to me an important omission, since the communicative pact is made explicit on a literal level, as the exhibition layout and communication strategy show, but not on a deeper level because it refuses to consider the effect that results from a series of underlying signification mechanisms, determinant in the comprehension of the analysed object, according to the principles of the generative semiotic. The risk is that of producing a dissonant effect, a sort of double bind where we are attracted by a specific point of view carrying specific values (Gonzales-Torres is the recognised symbol of freedom of thought, the courage of taking a gentle but strong position against all discrimination, being concerned with sexual preferences, ethnical origins, political orientation…) but the way we are invited to experience the generative effect of his work is proposed in a spatially controlled way, as we saw before, and even controlled on a communicational level in the mimetic retake of his work.

A second important example to which I would like to draw attention is the *Geschichten im Konflikt* exhibi-

***Geschichten in Konflikt,* installation view, Haus der Kunst, Munich 2012.**

tion held in celebration of its 75th anniversary. It is well known that the history of the Haus der Kunst is not a common history. This exhibition was not only an occasion to recall the history of a space, originally designed as an instrument for Nazi propaganda and, thus, the site of some of WWII's most tragic events, but also reveals that this history (and the exhibition that shows it) is the evidence of a path of enfranchisement, of a process of distancing the past, enabled by a concrete auto-reflexive view. Briefly, Haus der Kunst was erected where there once stood a glass and iron building built in the second half of the 19th century for the German *Große Berliner Gewerbeausstellung* (1896), then the place for art exhibitions and later a location for a kind of (art) fair which was eventually destroyed by fire in 1931. The construction of the new building, upon Hitler's request, as a place to affirm the Nazi idea of art, started in 1933 and ended in 1937.

The Haus der Kunst has been the location of seven editions of the *Große Deutsche Kunstausstellung*, and following WWII was occupied by the American army who turned it into an officer club with a restaurant, a dance hall and several shops. Jazz bands played and variety shows were performed in the "Hall of Honour". Exhibiting activities were revived again at the end of the 40s

Model of the Haus der Deutschen Kunst during the "Glanzzeiten deutscher Geschichte" parade, 1933.

and consisted of, at first, establishing relations between the historical avant-garde protagonists who had been persecuted as Entartete Kunst by the Nazis, and secondly, reactivating the link with the contemporary artistic debate until a relevant position in the international scene was re-established, thanks to the quality of the exhibiting programmes and the ability to intercept the agitation of present artistic debate.

The temporal arch narrated in the *Geschichten im Konflikt* exhibition stretches from the building's design/construction in 1937, also the year of Picasso's personal exhibition (and also when *Guernica* was shown, previously housed at the *Internationale de Arts et Techniques dans la Vie Moderne* in the Spanish pavilion in Paris, not far from the German pavilion displaying the model of the Haus der Kunst which at that time won the Gran Prix for architecture), to when the first edition of documenta was held in Kassel, that is, not until Germany re-enters the European and international cultural discourse.

Geschichten im Konflikt, supervised by Sabine Brantl and Ulrich Wilmes, designed by the Berlin architectural studio Elfe Erenler, with a six-part drama project supervised by artist Christian Philipp Müller (consisting of five parts inside the spaces of the building and one on the external wall, each autonomously implementing the observation points of the exhibited material or in other cases influencing the setting), was also introduced, during the days of the inauguration, by a conference that witnessed the participation of major scholars and artists, including Buchloh, Didi-Huberman, Mieke Bal, and Alfredo Jaar (to name just a few). Each detail of this exhibition deserves specific consideration, but in this paper I will concentrate on a work shown in the sixth and last section, dedicated to the period between 1946 and 1955, i.e., the restarting of the exhibiting activity, a period which is thoroughly documented and consultable via the dedicated booklet and archival material held by the exhibition as the conclusion to the itinerary. The work consists of a collection of white and black photographs taken by the German artist, Hans Haacke, who from 1956 studied at the Academia of Fine Arts in Kassel with Frits Winter, one of the most famous German abstract painters of that period, and who in 1959 was selected along with other students to work for documenta 2 as set assistant, guard and tour guide for the exhibition. From among the collection's nearly 300 photographs, Haacke selected 26 to compose a series entitled *Photographic Notes, documenta 2, 1959* (1959), shown for the first time at the *Stations of Modernism* (Berlinische Galerie, Berlin, 1988).

Hans Haacke, *Photographic Notes, documenta 2, 1959*, 1959.

This work represents an important moment in his career. *Photographic Notes* is the result of a focus on the relation between the public and the exhibited art work, as the attention to the background in his photos shows. In addition to a curiosity demonstrated for visitor typologies, faces, attitudes and movements and glimpses of the work exhibited in documenta 2, a further point of interest looked at how Haacke began to no longer consider works of art as isolated objects but instead as always related to the exhibition context: becoming a characteristic theme of his career.

Turning back to the fact that this work represented the conclusion of the exhibition, whose entire title was *Geschichten im Konflikt: Das Haus der Kunst und der ideologische Gebrauch von Kunst 1937-1955*, a first consideration is the fact that the title entails a precise date of conclusion, e.g. 1955, and that this photographic series was realised in 1959. If it is acceptable to believe that this incoherence is firmly not meant as an oversight, then I propose we consider expanding the temporal arch of the investigation exactly within this exception.

In trying to broaden the frame, we end up again focusing on the underlying mechanisms of signification that act in this exhibition. Which is the narrative model acting in this case? What does the exhibition say? Who is speaking through it besides artists and curators?

I believe it is not possible to establish what the rules are that fix the balance of powers between institutions and the subjects who play decisional roles therein (museum institutions vs. curators). I think they get redefined along with the context. In the case of the Biennale of Istanbul (which has seen its 13th edition) there have always been

curators who have had the opportunity to build exhibitions characterised by their vision.
This allows them a wider action space compared, for example, to those who supervise the Biennale of Venice, and certainly wider compared to those curators acting inside an institution because continuity simply allows for repetitions and continuity, which broaden perspective, whereas the supervision of a single exhibition does not. It is in this sense that in reference to the Biennale of Istanbul I consider of minor importance the role of the institution, in comparison to the role of the curators, in the realization of the exhibition. In the case of the Haus der Kunst the situation is evidently different, due furthermore to its being not only an exhibition which represents the anniversary of the institution but also an exhibition focused on the history of the institution itself. In this sense the tale narrated by the curators, in collaboration with the varied contributors of the exhibition's realization, cannot but coincide with that of the institution. Said differently, there must have been a substantial agreement between the parts and, having seen the conditions, I believe it could not have been different. Based on this assumption, the question asked before resembles at some level the exhibition's title itself, but at a deeper level it might perhaps have been transformed in the question, which draws on the generative semiotic of "What is the self-narration proposed by the institution through the choices of the curator?". If this reasoning makes sense, we might perhaps start to reconstruct a tale which starts from a situation where negative forces are playing (Hitler, Nazism), and through a series of passages attains a very positive situation as the present one (Haus der Kunst as an open institution able to intercept central issues of the international artistic debate); that is, it would be a *mise-en-scène* of a transformation process, from the darkness of the first years to the positivity of present time, with the effect on the spectator of a proper happy ending. But if the happy ending concerns the present time, the tale of the exhibition starts more than fifty years ago, in 1955, the year of Picasso, of *Guernica,* and of the first edition of documenta. Why then add a single incoherent contribution to that date? It is true that if the first edition of

documenta was focused on giving back to art the dignity and the attention Nazism refused it, then the second edition realigned itself with the debate of the time, and this realignment might be accounted for by a single work. If that is indeed the case, the Haacke photographic series would find its legitimacy. In this regards, however, one of Haake's texts – originally a paper presented at the conference *Landmark Exhibitions: Contemporary Art Shows Since 1968*, published in the on-line magazine *Tate Papers*, (n. 12, 2009) – suggests the possibility of adding some significant element. Haacke retraces the main stages of his work from his education up to his latest works, but proceeding with that caution needed when dealing with accounts I try to consider two of the relevant points this text entails. The introduction is enlightening: "As an introduction, let me speak about how I lost my innocence as a starry-eyed art student in Kassel in 1959" (ibid.), that is, when, being a student in Kassel, he worked at the documenta edition and took those pictures that became a part of the *Geschichten im Konflikt* exhibition. Then he lingers on the German artistic context of the time and this is how he describes his experience at documenta 2:

> As sometimes bewildered or awed onlookers, we got a sense that this exhibition was not just an art event but had national and even international political implications. As was to be expected, local dignitaries like the mayor of Kassel and the governor of the state of Hessen attended the opening. However, the president of the Republic came, too, as did cabinet members of the Federal government and ambassadors from many countries. As I learned later, the CIA had sponsored my first encounter with abstract expressionist paintings at documenta 2. Ironically, while having to fend off McCarthyite accusations against these works, it was the Museum of Modern Art's International Council that sent them on a European tour to serve as weapons in the Cold War (ibid.).

Today this fact is recognised, but historically this awareness constituted the loss of innocence cited by Haacke, that is, the contact – still as a student – with the complexity of the art world and its complicity with power. We should remember that in 1993 the same artist, invited to Venice to represent Germany, realised a pavilion with an uneven floor and with an entrance where the German mark was reproduced together with a picture of Hitler visiting the Biennale of 1937. The event did not represent a scandal for Germany, but rather was a confirmation of its willingness to uphold a constant confrontation with its past. And the choice to insert his photographic series, which indeed shows another passage where images (pictures of American expressionists in documenta 2) are used in an ideological sense, might express the same intention. Surely the ideology is not the same, but of course the pressure exercised by the United States on Europe, also through the works of these artists, still had a pervasive effect. To paraphrase what David Joselit (2003) wrote – abstract expressionists were able to interpret this mood – before and even better than pop artists – in a period when the tragic falls of European totalitarianism went together with Stalin's regime, that is, when individualism acquired a kind of moral and political nature. Putting into the public sphere the (individualistic) need of their artistic action – according to Joselit – beyond their intentions, they made a strong contribution to the construction of the consumer, an individualist character itself whose main ability is being able to choose (products). This trace, beyond the fact that it will result in a fact, does not undermine but rather modifies and widens the discourse. The positive result does not end in the international positioning of the Haus der Kunst but, in revealing Hans Haacke's work, shows a further ideological use of art, confirmed in his text. This widens and draws closer in time the positive result assimilating it with the gaining of an auto-reflexive identity, an additional value far more unique and exclusive than internationalization.
I do not know if it is possible to reach a conclusion at the end of this exercise, that is, the attempt to present such complex devices as indeed art exhibitions are, to grasp the interaction between different levels, also between

the most invisible ones, working with tools arising from semiotic and communication studies. It is an exercise about opposing a resistance to superficial interpretations. Perhaps it is all this together. It might be nothing new, but the importance of such exercises does not belong to their novelty but to repeating them, seeking to increase the precision and efficacy of what we are doing.

References

Baxandall M. (1991), Exhibiting Intention: Some Preconditions of the Visual Display of Culturally Purposeful Objects, in Karp I. S., Lavine D. (ed.), *Exhibiting Culture,* Smithsonian Press, Washington D.C.

Bourdieu P. (1979), *La Distinction. Critique sociale du jugement,* Les Editions du Minuit; Eng. trans. *Distinction: A Social Critique of the Judgement of Taste,* Harvard University Press, Cambridge (MA), 1984.

Brantl S., Wilmes U. (2012), *Geschichten im Konflikt,* Booklet of the Exhibition, Haus der Kunst, Münich.

Buchloh B. (2012), Farewell to an Identity, *Artforum,* December, pp. 252-263.

Carmagnola F. (2009), *La fabbrica del desiderio,* Lupetti, Milano.

Foster H. (2011), *The Art-Architecture Complex,* Verso, London/New York.

Haacke H. (2009), Lessons Learned. Landmark Exhibitions: Contemporary Art Shows Since 1968, *Tate Papers,* issue 12, autumn, www.tate.org.uk/research/publications/tate-papers/lessons-learned [28.11.2012]

Jakobson R. (1963), *Essais de linguistique générale,* Editions de Minuit, Paris.

Jameson F. (1984), Postmodernism, or The Cultural Logic of Late Capitalism, *New Left Review* n. 146, July August, pp. 59-92.

Joselit D. (2003), *American Art since 1945,* Thames and Hudson, London/New York.

Koolhas R. (2002), *The Harvard Design School Guide to Shopping/ Harvard Design School Project on the City 2,* Taschen, Köln.

Krauss R. (1990), The Cultural Logic of the Late Capitalist Museum, *October,* Vol. 54 (Autumn, 1990), pp. 3-17.

Pine J. B. Gilmore J. H. (1999), *The Experience Economy: Work Is Theater & Every Business a Stage,* Harvard Business School Press, Cambridge (MA).

Rifkin J. (2000), *The Age of Access: The New Culture of Hypercapitalism, Where all of Life is a Paid-For Experience,* Tarcher, Los Angeles.

Warhol A. (1975), *The Philosophy of Andy Warhol (From A to B & Back Again),* Harcourt Brace Jovanovich, New York.

DESIGNING EXHIBITIONS
Something Fantastic – Julian Schubert

I am going to describe our approach to designing exhibitions and exhibiting architecture with four examples of our latest practice. I am going to connect each exhibition with a claim that was guiding that particular design. The four claims are important for each design and could be our guideline for a fantastic exhibition: because architecture and urban planning affects everybody, we respect the audience *and address non-professionals as well as professionals; as exhibitions are mostly temporary, we* use minimal means *for the installation; we* embrace the spirit *of the exhibited projects and we try to* create a sensation.

Respect the audience! – Cidade de Deus 2032 at Studio X in Rio de Janeiro, June 2012

While Rio+20 was running in Rio de Janeiro in June 2012, the project space of Columbia University located at Praca Tiradentes – Studio X – wanted to display the research and design projects of students of the MAS ETH Zurich[1] within a seminar dealing with *Urban Mutations on the Edge* in general and, since 2012, with Brazilian informality in specific. The focus of the to-be-exhibited semester was the infamous neighbourhood Cidade de Deus in Rio de Janeiro.

Cidade de Deus undoubtedly has problems, not least its image, as depicted in the 1996 novel by Paulo Lins and in the 2002 well-known movie *City of God*. But apart from insufficient infrastructure and, consequently, the apparent pollution, the urgencies of Cidade de Deus have shifted. After the pacification in 2009 – which means that military police marched in to expel the area of weapons and drugs, to install a permanent presence and to clear the ground for civil services like schools, or subsidised restaurants – access to health care, reliable supply of energy, affordable houses, sanitary minimums, and connection to public transport began to replace murders, drugs, and violence. The neighbourhood seems pleasant

1 The Master of Advanced Studies at Eidgenössische Technische Hochschule Zurich runs as a one-year programme and is chaired by Prof. Marc Àngelil.

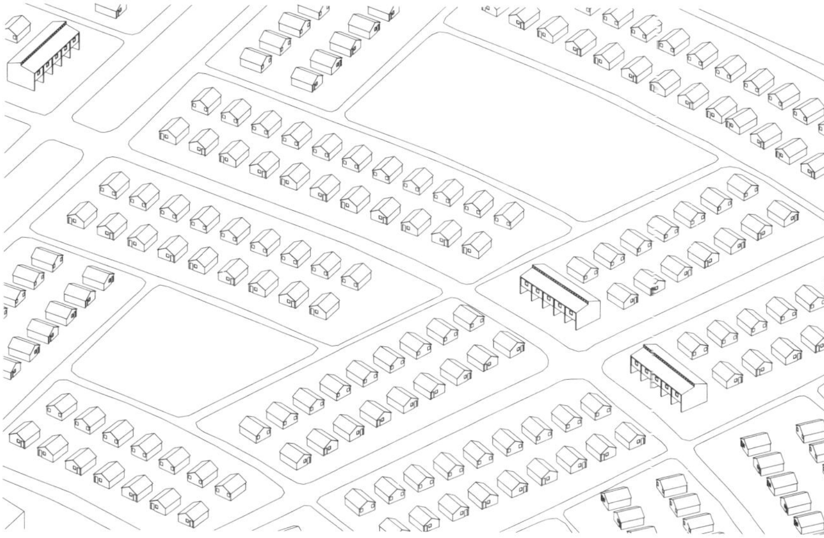

Cidade de Deus 1960,
isometric view, 2012.

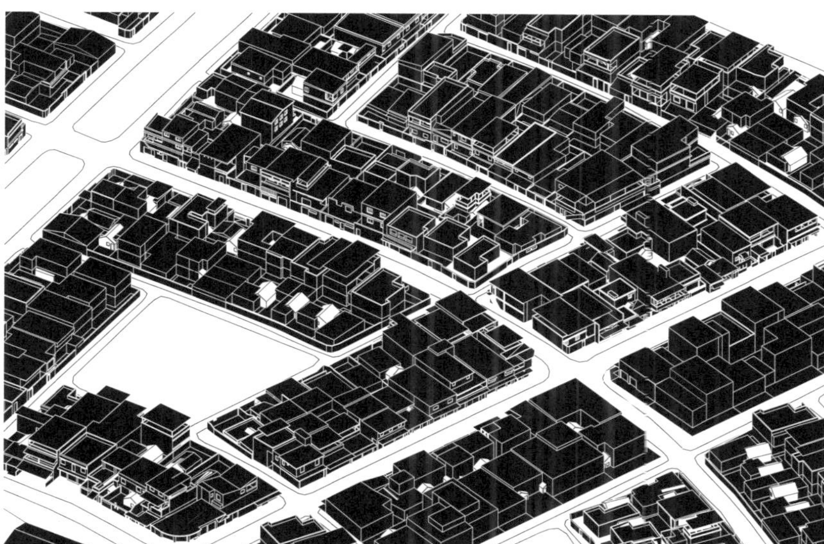

Cidade de Deus 2012,
isometric view, 2012.

nowadays, characterised by the hand-painted graphics scattered all over the place, its mostly car-free streets filled with people and playing children, busy areas with shops and restaurants and more quiet areas with only housing, public squares with soccer fields or open-air gyms.

The questions the university course asked when looking at Cidade de Deus were: "How did this settlement grow into what it is now and what personal and social arrangements lie behind its spatial formulation?". Firstly, Cidade de Deus is not a favela[2]. It looks like a favela, but it is a formally planned development that grew through informal extensions and self-construction into what it is now. It was built in the early 1960s outside the city as a settlement for poor people and was financed by the US as part of an American-Brazilian alliance to establish a Brazilian middle class – a middle class that buys refrigerators, cars, sofas, etc. The development consisted of 3,000 single family houses and 500 apartment units in various 5-storey buildings. Now it houses between 38,000 and 70,000 inhabitants depending on the sources you trust[3]. Some elements of the original urban layout resisted the densification and are still recognisable, but most parts were adapted to the needs of its inhabitants to an extent that makes the original plan unidentifiable.

The task of the exhibition was to show the existing situation as well as the course's design proposals that prescribe informal growth as a strategy for future development. As Cidade de Deus for Brazilians seems a domain for the task force of the military police, or NGOs, but not as a topic for architectural discourse – which is still dominated by the seducing elegance of Brazilian modernism – the main goal of the exhibition was to shift the general public's perception of favelas and to start a

2 A favela describes a settlement that is erected on land that does not belong to the settler. The name comes from the plant Favela which was brought back to Rio de Janeiro from North Eastern Brazil by soldiers who were sent there to stop riots. When they returned, they were without land or rights and had to build their houses on state-owned land.

3 The municipality or Rio de Janeiro counts 36,000 inhabitants, the community organisation Associação de Moradores União Comunitária Cidade de Deus counts 70,000.

discussion on the possible benefits of informal architecture. As the exhibition took place at the same time as the Rio+20 conference, we presented Cidade de Deus as the winner of a fictitious competition, the *Cidade Maravilhosa Award 2032* (Rio+20+20). This allowed us to show research and projects as highlights of Cidade de Deus, which, in 2032, might both be realistic. In reference to street signs we found that in Cidade de Deus the dominating means of communication was colourful posters. In the exhibition projects were not shown as the work of professionals, with abstract plans and sections, but as collages, photographs, axonometric views, or objects that reveal spatial, architectural and urban qualities of favelas which haven't been visible before due to the focus on social problems. Objects and two large models were displayed on a market stand-like table made from *cavaletes,* the table stands that are used by Rio's street vendors. Along with the exhibition we organised a workshop that brought together – with the help of the NGO Catalytic Communities – architecture students from Rio's architecture and urban planning university FAU UFRJ and inhabitants of Cidade de Deus to discuss more ideas based on the proposals and findings that were on display. I cannot evaluate the responses on the exhibition, but the NGO's feedback for the workshops was that they had never seen so lively and open a correspondence among participants. Especially for people living in favelas, urban planning usually means the danger that their house is on the list of houses that for whatever reason have to be demolished. Understandably, there are certain concerns towards planners and we think – or hope – that the visual language that we used, and that did not come across as a piece of academic research to be consumed but instead as an engaging approach in a language of popular local culture, helped people to start thinking on their own.

Cidade de Deus 2032, exhibition's poster in the streets of Complexo Alemao, 2012.

Use minimal means – Raumproduktion at Kunsthalle Düsseldorf, Summer 2011

Raumproduktion was an art exhibition curated by Matthias Böttger. It was a group show of different artistic positions to the simple question: "How is space created?" Several artists were invited to either create a site-specific installation or show an existing piece. The list of exhibited pieces was manifold, from an on-site wall painting by Alex Schwedter-La to large sculptures by Larissa Fassler. Not all works were present from the first day of the show because Böttger wanted to successively fill the space with more works by announcing an open call to befriended artists. Like a sketchbook, the pages would be filled over time, and the same was literally to happen to the catalogue as well. So the task was to design a layout that worked for the two dimensions of the book as well as the three dimensions of the museum and that would be rigid and ordered enough to cope with the project's flexibility and diversity.

We decided to translate an element common in graphic design into a spatial framework: the guidelines, those thin lines used in page layout software that help you position an object in a document. Instead of modifying the space with partitioning walls and physically creating rooms, we stretched a grid of strings into the hall. The whole room became a book, each segment a page. Differently from a book, where you have to leaf through the pages and the whole of the book cannot be grasped in one sweeping glance, the visitor was able to perceive the room in its entirety and also see relations between things that hung next to each other which, in a book, would have to be on different pages. The grid of strings combined two elements of book design: formally, it represented the Van de Graaf canon, which was devised in the early 19th century for discovering the geometric patterns which Gutenberg used in the 14th century to create harmonic page divisions. This canon was redrawn with strings as a layer floating several centimetres in front of the longest wall, the edges of the 'pages' were extruded into the space as strings reaching to the other side of the room. In terms of colour, it resembled the neon coloured guides of the layout software Adobe InDesign. As thin

Raumproduktion, test for the installation, 2011.

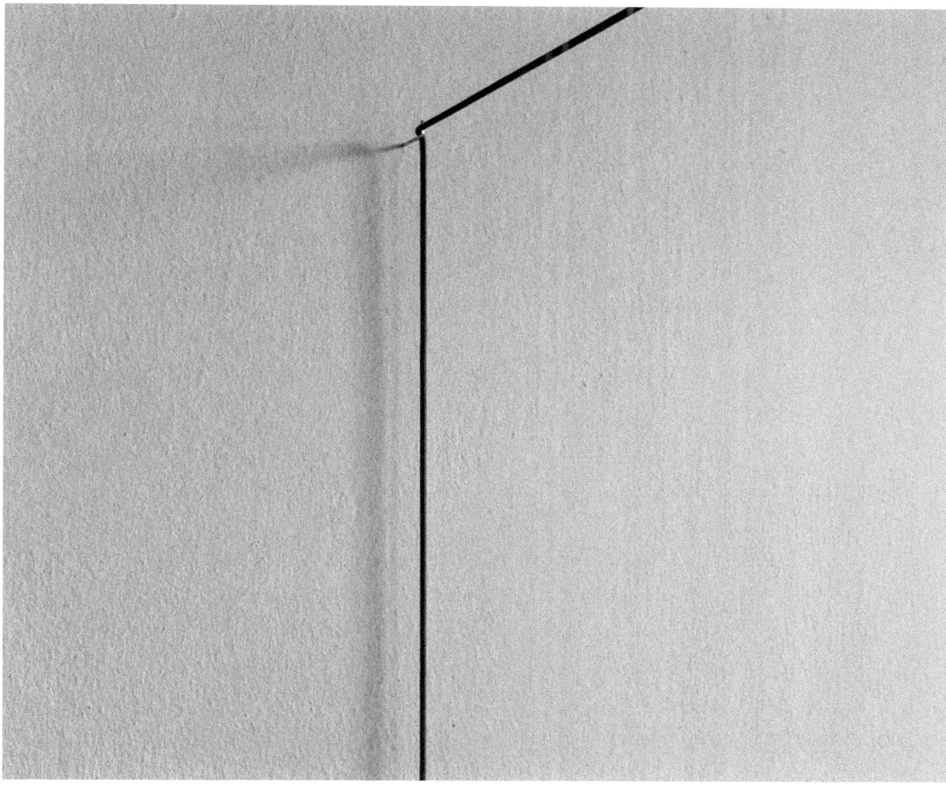

Raumproduktion, **test for the installation, 2011.**

colourful strings crisscrossing the room at a height of 30 cm, it looked like a skillfully made tripping hazard instead of an exhibition in a public art museum. We used two hundred Graphen cubes – roughly 5 x 5 x 5 cm – from a junkyard as weights to hold down the strings. A bucket of one hundred cubes held the string construction in tension. Finally, the installation not only paid tribute to the fact that other people could later on place something in the exhibition without consulting us or the curator, because they could easily spot the blank 'pages' on the wall in which to place their work, but it also – and even more exceptionally – remained significantly under the budget. The total cost of all the material for the installation was only 30 Euros, including nails, strings and shipping. We paid more, around 90 Euros, for the 1:1 tests beforehand, in searching for the right strings.

Machen!, model of the exhibition setting, 2012.

***Machen!*, installation view, Aedes Architecture Forum, Berlin, 2012.**

Embrace the spirit – *Machen!* at Aedes Gallery Berlin, September 2012

In September 2012 we designed an exhibition about the six winning projects of a prize rewarded by the Holcim Foundation for Sustainable Construction. The exhibition took place at Aedes Gallery in Berlin. The exhibited projects were the Smart Material House by Barkow Leibinger, the Training Centre for Sustainability by Anna Heringer, Martin Rauch, Elmar Naegele and Ernst Waibel with Salima Naji, The Collège de Gando by Kére Architecture, the Earthen School by Ziegert Roswag Seiler, the Low2NO project by Sauerbruch Hutton and the Flussbad project by realities:united. As the displayed projects showed how construction materials can be used more efficiently, or how to build with recycled materials, or how to create a public pool with a filter system, it was even more important to us to avoid what for temporary installations, like exhibitions, almost always counts: that they are installed with resources and material that after the short life of the exhibition become a pile of trash.

The exhibition before ours was designed by Atelier Bow-Wow. Luckily, they had made some beautiful and

Druot, Lacaton & Vassal, Transformation eines 60er Jahre Wohnhochhauses, installation view, Deutsches Architekturmuseum, Frankfurt, 2012.

Druot, Lacaton & Vassal, Transformation eines 60er Jahre Wohnhochhauses, view of the exhibition model for DAM, Frankfurt, 2012.

Druot, Lacaton & Vassal, Transformation eines 60er Jahre Wohnhochhauses, view of the exhibition model for DAZ, Berlin, 2013.

Druot, Lacaton & Vassal, Transformation eines 60er Jahre Wohnhochhauses, installation view, DAM, Frankfurt, 2012.

decent alterations to the lighting, singular bulbs instead of professional lighting systems, and displayed their plans on tables fixed onto standard IKEA stands. We decided to go for a direct recycling and to re-use the materials left after this exhibition. The only things we had to buy were some extra IKEA stands to create signs that would make these a more dominant feature of the installation. The rest involved simply moving the tables from a scattered arrangement to one big table where big models were displayed. Another lucky circumstance was that five of the six exhibited offices were based in Berlin and it was easy to collect the models in one afternoon. We decided to display the original panels handed in by the architects for the competition. This generated a further information layer to the content of the show: the possibility of seeing the different layouts handed in allowed the visitor to make comparisons among them and to form a personal opinion about how a project has to be submitted in order to win a competition. For the graphics – which were used for both the exhibition and the accompanying catalogue – we went for quite a strict and bold appearance with big red frames to avoid an improvised look and to introduce something obviously different to the Atelier Bow Wow exhibition. In order to be free enough not to plan everything beforehand, but instead to react and work with the situation at hand, requires some fixed anchor points, in this case the graphic design.

Create a sensation – Druot Lacaton Vassal: Tour Bois le Prêtre at DAM Frankfurt, September 2012, and DAZ Berlin, January 2013

When Ilka and Andreas Ruby asked us to collaborate with them in the exhibition of the project of Anne Lacaton, Jean-Philippe Vassal and Philippe Drout for the tower Bois Le Pretre in Paris, we were very honoured. The project to us seemed to be the incarnation of a new approach to architecture, one that is summed up quite nicely by Lacaton & Vassal's manifesto at the entrance of the exhibition, a part of which read: "It's a question of never demolishing, never removing or replacing, but always adding, transforming and using." They call their approach the PLUS principle, creating more space by investing fewer resources, be they financial or material. Lacaton, Vassal and Druot did not replace the existing tower from the 1960s – which, as in many *banlieues* of Paris, the French government wanted to tear down with the argument that the buildings and urban planning would be responsible for social problems – but instead convinced the owner to invest the resources into the old building by way of extending it. The most important step was to add a new façade, consisting of a winter garden two metres in depth and a balcony one metre in depth. The architects call it a thermal insulation you can live in. The result is light rooms, incredible views, a gradual blending of inside and outside, and also happy inhabitants as they could all stay in the building while the renovation process took place.

One reference we used to develop our concept of the show was that of exhibitions of early Modernists that aimed at showing wide audience how modern apartments should be furnished and how modern people were supposed to live or other exhibitions, for example, the *Neues Wohnen* exhibition by the German Werkbund. These exhibitions were 1:1 installations that would make the experience of visiting them less intellectual and more sensual. Visitors could not only see the functional furniture and the open plans represented on paper, but they could walk inside them or sit on them. The answer to the question of how can architecture make life better, posed by Lacaton, Vassal and Druot and answered in their project for the Tour Bois Le Pretre is – for us – similarly revolutionary. No more sparely lit rooms that create isolating climates which are independent from the outside, but instead an experience of living with the seasons, the sun, the rain. In interviews published in the catalogue accompanying the exhibition, inhabitants talk about how much more they are aware of natural phenomena now, how much more they appreciate sunshine, growing plants, birds singing, etc. In all the images made by Philippe Ruault and Frederic Druot upon completion of the project, you see how people plant pots with flowers, herbs or small trees, how their apartments get furnished with garden furniture and so on.

For the sensual experience, which we wanted to give

to the visitors, we created a wallpaper of Ruault and Druot's images as high as the original rooms of the Tour Bois Le Pretre. We cropped the images so that eye level would always be at 1.6 meters and to make the illusion of really being in the Tour Bois le Prêtre for a visitor who is standing in the exhibition as real as possible. We furnished the exhibition room with common furniture that you would also see on the images. The project itself is not about a design language, or exclusive furniture as some pieces were bought on eBay and most of them were rented theatre equipment. We also rented plants, lots of potted plants. We placed the items so that certain views in the museum created the illusion of really being in Paris, in a tower, in that other way of living. The complete explanation of the project was on another *layer:* in Frankfurt we installed an office inside the *house in a house* that Oswald Mathias Ungers had built in the centre of the DAM, the German Architecture Museum where the exhibition took place, and in Berlin there was an explanation pin-board at the entrance – in order not to disturb the sensual, non-intellectual, experience that we wanted to create with this exhibition.

ARCHITECTURAL ALLUSIONS

Ilka & Andreas Ruby

Architecture can't be exhibited. At least not in the way you can exhibit art, where you can show a painting or a sculpture, i.e. the thing itself. In architecture the thing, the building, is usually too big to fit in any conventional exhibition space; it already sits in its proper exhibition space - its site. Whenever we exhibit architecture in museums, we have to decrease its scale, translate its materiality, and impoverish its synesthetic definition to visual or audio information only. Ultimately, these are just translations of architecture; they can only provide allusions to the real thing. The aspect that we find fascinating about exhibiting architecture is the impossibility of actually representing architecture – it presents both a challenge and an opportunity to push architecture exhibitions in new, and perhaps more effective, directions.

Statue of Liberty under construction, Paris, 1883.

The main problem with exhibiting architecture is that the subject – the building – does not fit the enclosed space of a museum or gallery, simply because it is too big. The picture of the Statue of Liberty being built in Paris before it was gifted to America represents the incompatibility between the two scales of a building and an interior space: architecture cannot exist and at the same time contain itself because there is a collision of scale and of meaning. Maybe this is not so bad after all, though, because architecture exhibits itself. When we walk through a city we come to understand it by its buildings. They tell stories about the building process and about the cultural sensitivity of a place and time. They tell us a lot by what things they show; they also hide.

Architecture cannot be exhibited like art. Despite this, architecture curators could learn a thing or two from conceptual art of the 60s and land art, which focused on the materiality and the scale of artworks because they, like buildings, were also too big to fit in any exhibition space. Land art, which declared natural phenomena as works of art, had to transcend the exhibition space; land art was therefore created and exhibited outside the studio and the gallery, in the natural landscape, where it was left to change and erode under natural conditions.

The American land artist Robert Smithson eventually worked his way back into the exhibition space with a series of non-site specific work, in which he took materials that were *out there* and brought them back into the gallery. When we curate exhibitions on architecture, we like to focus on the process of translating the subject into something that can be exhibited in an enclosed space. We try to come to terms with the fact that what we're exhibiting is not the *real thing,* but just an allusion to it. Like the French philosopher Jean Francois Lyotard once said, we have to overcome the idea that we can represent reality because its most important aspects very often cannot be represented (1984). We can at best allude and link to them, which is the way we approach the task of exhibiting architecture. Three methods of curating architecture, which we have termed *Mind Game, Body Check,* and *Trompe l'Oeil,* help us allude to architecture.

1. Mind Game

In 1968, Bruce Nauman exhibited the *Concrete Tape Recorder Piece,* a piece that consisted of a tape recorder stuck inside a block of concrete. The spectator was told that the tape recorder, which was plugged in to the wall, played the sounds of someone screaming; however, the spectator could neither hear the scream nor see the actual tape recorder, as it was completely sealed off with concrete. The work of art could therefore not be experienced phenomenologically, but only as a *mind game* that forced the spectator to think about the piece, rather than focus on the mute object. Creating a mind game that prioritizes the concept of architecture in the place of its experience is one strategy with which curators can address the absence of architecture.

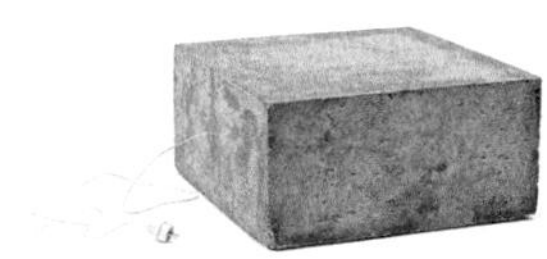

Bruce Nauman, *Concrete tape recorder piece,* 1968.

We applied the *Mind Game* strategy to architecture in 2003 when we curated *Cross-Atmosphering,* a small exhibition on the work of the Slovenian office Sadar + Vuga in Salon Blauraum. By that point, Sadar + Vuga had realised almost a dozen buildings on different scales, which we wanted to display with one image and one story per project. Rather than writing standard architectural descriptions of the projects, the stories we wrote were all invented based on certain social trends that we had

As rising life expectancies shift the distribution of the population towards older ages, there is increasing demand among the elderly for new ways of living. Freed from professional and familial obligations, retirees are moving back into the city in droves, attracted by possibilities to spend their free time productively and develop connections with people their own age. The retirement community Vita Activa responds to this trend. Apartments of various sizes and plans are arranged towards the back of the building, while the front façade presents a multitude of service functions, including a medical clinic, a physical therapy practice, a multimedia library, as well as a performance space. A restaurant with outdoor seating and a bar occupies the penthouse story. A roomy fitness center, on the other hand, can be found on the basement level – transparent skylights provide a luminous accent to the concrete plaza in front of the building. The various functions of the building are connected by a multistory entrance hall, which also offers a space for spontaneous interaction between tenants and seniors from the larger community flocking to the center to take part in its dynamic (yet age-appropriate) lifestyle.

***Cross Atmosphering*, image and story for one of the exhibited buildings, Salon Blauraum, Hamburg, 2003.**

observed in Slovenia. We wrote them while looking at the images of the buildings, putting aside what we already know about the projects and instead imagining, based on their architectural atmospheres, what they could be – maybe an elderly home, a new high-speed train, a studio for a late-night talk show, a climbing hall, a sports hall, an aquarium, a new IKEA, a playground for children, a new Jacuzzi, a yoga studio, etc.

These stories and photographs were exhibited on a wall by the entrance, which was covered with posters pinned on a cork wall as if it were a big pin-up board. Nothing suggested that anything was out of the ordinary. It was only when the spectator entered deeper in the exhibition space that the true programmes and stories behind the buildings were unveiled. Here, in a second hallway-like room, we showed plans, sections and images explaining the projects in greater detail (nowhere in the exhibition did it specify what was true and what wasn't, but the nature and detail of these boards suggested that they were non-fictional). The visitors searched for the buildings that they had read about by the entrance; when they found them, they were surprised to find other programmatic elements than they were expecting (such as a swimming pool, for example). This sparked a discussion among the curious visitors, who slowly began to realise that the stories that they had read were fictional. This mind game raised questions about the function of architecture: how do people use architecture? Can this function change if the buildings stay the same?

The most interesting response to *Cross-Atmosphering* was that most of the visitors expressed to us that they liked the fictional stories more than the project's true descriptions. At the end, they left the exhibition taking two versions of each building with them. The exhibition in this way worked like the *Vertical Earth Kilometre,* Walter de Maria's contribution to documenta 6 in Kassel.

The piece consists of a brass rod that supposedly extends a kilometre into the earth. Like with Nauman's *Concrete Tape Recorder Piece,* the viewer cannot be certain that the rod actually reaches a kilometre depth or that there's a rod at all; all he or she can see is the end of the rod, which lies flush with the surface of the earth and might as well be a two-inch diameter coin that's set into the ground. Because there is no way of verifying the veracity of the piece, it lives only in the mind of the viewer; the reality of the art work is produced by the narrative that the artist has created and not its physical presence.

2. Body Check

In 2009, we contributed a video installation called *Endless Bauhaus* to the blockbuster exhibition *Bauhaus: A Conceptual Model* at the Martin Gropius Bau in Berlin.

For the exhibition, the interior space of the Martin Gropius Bau was divided into two main spaces. A gallery, which wrapped around a central atrium, exhibited a historical perspective on the Bauhaus, its furniture, architecture and so on. We were invited, along with artist Christine Hill, to contribute an installation about how the Bauhaus is received today, which would be exhibited in the atrium. With our installation, which comprised a seating area where exhibition visitors could sit, relax, and watch a video, we wanted to challenge the institutionalization of the Bauhaus. The video consisted of us interviewing eleven contemporary designers and architects about their thoughts on the Bauhaus. The most important aspect of the final video was that the interviewees' responses and feelings toward the Bauhaus varied radically and often even conflicted with one another. If the overall exhibition tried to present a coherent *conceptual model,* the video installation tried to problematize a contemporary tendency to pigeonhole the Bauhaus. The name of the school Bauhaus suggests that it was united behind one firm agenda and ideology, which was not the case; the Bauhaus was and continues to be what you make of it. In fact, the school encouraged debate and fostered different approaches under the three chairs of Walter Gropius, Hannes Meyer, and Ludwig Mies van der Rohe. By editing the videos so that it seemed like the interviewees were reacting to each other, even though they were interviewed independently of each other, the video re-enacted the intellectual debate of the Bauhaus, an important legacy that has since been forgotten.

A second important aspect of our installation, which is part of the *Body Check* strategy, was the simple fact that

Bauhaus, a conceptual model, installation view with Endless Bauhaus, Martin Gropius Bau, Berlin, 2009.

it provided seating to the viewers. For us, *Body Check* is a way to challenge the institutional protocols and atmosphere of galleries and museums by focusing on the visitor's experience of a space. As is to be expected of anything Bauhaus-related, the exhibition included a lot of chairs, which the visitors could not sit on because they were displayed on pedestals and shelves; they are also, of course, much too valuable. We wanted to highlight the fact that the curators of an exhibition on Bauhaus – a movement that aimed to create something practical and affordable to the common man – had not considered how absurd it would have been if a show filled with chairs offered no seating to the public. Looking at this seemingly never-ending archive of chairs must wear down the visitors, who would at some point probably like to sit down somewhere. Our installation and Hill's gave them a chance to do so.

Olafur Eliasson, *Weather Project*, 2003.

Exhibitions should allow visitors to respond intuitively to a space and the objects within it; they should encourage visitors to spontaneously and naturally engage with what's on display. Olafur Eliasson's famously accomplished this with his *The Weather Project* for the Tate Modern, in which he created a sun-like installation in the Turbine Hall. On feeling the warm glow of the *sun*, the visitors to the Tate appropriated the Turbine Hall's concrete floor as their beach. It was beautiful to observe visitors transgress what's considered *normal behaviour* in a gallery and museum. They had found their own way to engage with the art in the same way that the loveable, romantic Monsieur Hulot in the film *Mon Oncle* by Jacques Tati comes to term with his sister's modern design sensibility; in one scene, Monsieur Hulot, after a long night at the pub, finds a way to make himself comfortable on his sister's impersonal and uncomfortable modern sofa by turning it upside down and transforming it into a chaise longue.

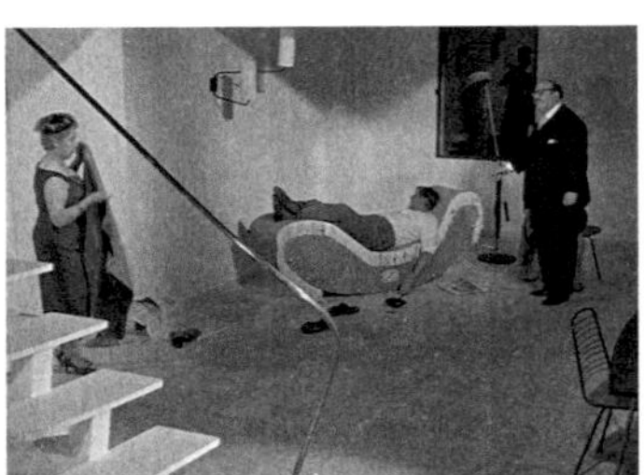

Jaques Tati, *Mon Oncle*, 1958.

The colours of the pillows depict the Bauhaus colour wheel in linear gradients. The exhibition designers who had proposed this idea wanted to represent the Bauhaus colour wheel very concretely, and we accepted to use the colours on the condition that the pillows would not be fixed in place and could therefore be moved around.

Druot, Lacaton & Vassal, Transformation eines 60er Jahre Wohnhochhauses, **installation view, DAM, Frankfurt, 2012.**

Again, the colour wheel is one of those normative ideas produced and perpetuated by the Bauhaus that we wanted to play with and make a little livelier and more approachable. So we introduced a little disorder to the colour wheel by displacing some of the colours and allowing the viewers to move the pillows around. In the end, this produced a map of how people had used the space. It also introduced some life to the exhibition and reflected our initial idea that the Bauhaus model is not fixed to one historical meaning, but open to multiple interpretations and applications.

3. Trompe l'Oeil

If architecture cannot fit in a gallery, then why not dissolve the boundaries of that gallery? This is what we attempted to do with the traveling Druot, Lacaton & Vassal exhibition, which was first shown at the Deutsches Architekturmuseum (DAM) in Frankfurt in 2012. The subject of the exhibition is the transformation of Tour Bois-le-Pretre, a run-down 1960s high rise that French architects Anne Lacaton, Jean-Philippe Vassal, and Frédéric Druot saved from the wrecking ball.

Druot, Lacaton & Vassal, Transformation eines 60er Jahre Wohnhochhauses, installation view, DAM, Frankfurt, 2012.

They proposed a very simple alternative to demolishing the building and rebuilding it – to tear down only the old asbestos-contaminated façade and substitute it with a new, inhabitable façade comprising a two-meter deep winter garden and a balcony. Replacing the façade took no longer than a week for each apartment and transformed this previously sad high rise into a desirable living space that was not only sunnier but also larger. The living space had increased by 40% following the retrofit; despite this, the building now consumes 60% less energy.
For the first time, residents could profit from the view that comes with living on the 14th floor in the 17th arrondissement in Paris, in a 120-sqm apartment that costs only 700 Euros per month.
There are many compelling aspects about the transformation Tour Bois-le-Pretre: it cost only half of what was expected for the demolition-and-reconstruction alternative and the inhabitants could remain in their apartments during most of the transformation. However, what we wanted to capture with this exhibition was the feeling that the inhabitants must have felt when they first returned to their apartments after the refurbishment – this extraordinary sense of a space becoming larger and extending beyond the walls of one's home.
But how do you exhibit these qualities in the DAM? Designed by O. M. Ungers, the DAM's exhibition spaces are charismatic but also very stiff. A house-like form occupies the middle of the exhibition space, which is divided into three floors. On the top floor, where we exhibited, the ceilings of balconies around the central *house* are very high and the space around the *house* is extremely tight. We have a lot of respect for this building, but we always pitied the curators who had to develop shows for its exhibition spaces.
In the case of our exhibition, which we conceived and realized together with Something Fantastic, this was different. The space by Ungers actually turned out to be a blessing. We discovered that the plan of the DAM is in fact very similar to that of the retrofitted Tour Bois-le-Pretre. There is an inner core – the house within the building – and then there is an in-between space between the house and the building's outer walls, like the

Druot, Lacaton & Vassal, *Transformation eines 60er Jahre Wohnhochhauses*, installation view, DAM, Frankfurt, 2012.

winter-garden spaces in the Tour Bois-le-Pretre. Then, of course, there is the space that is located beyond the outer walls. In the Tour Bois-le-Pretre this would be Paris, as seen through the buildings floor-to-ceiling glazed doors. This gave us the idea of wallpapering the outer walls of the exhibition space with 1:1 images, taken by Philippe Ruault looking out and through the winter gardens of Tour Bois-le-Pretre. We also placed furniture, plants, and other objects of daily use in front of the wallpaper to give the spectator the sensation of being inside an apartment. The effect of this trompe l'oeil was that even though exhibition space was fairly small, it appeared much bigger; like with the transformation of the Tour Bois-le-Pretre, the wallpapering made the horizon seem further away from the viewer. In addition, in photographs taken in front of the wallpaper it becomes difficult to tell where the three-dimensional objects scattered around the exhibition and the two-dimensional represented space meet. If you crop the image so that the background of the wallpaper fits the screen of the camera, then it looks like the photograph was taken in Paris. The visitors quickly understood this and almost immediately began posing for pictures in the space. Because we wanted the space around the *house* to create the same special sensation as a space that is somehow expanding, we decided to limit all technical information relating to the transformation to the exhibition catalogue, of which copies were scattered throughout the exhibition. Inside the *house,* we installed an architecture office that was used by a graduate of the Städelschule. She used the office to display how she had applied a similar retrofitting technique on a building in Frankfurt, which we hoped would start a conversation about how the Tour Bois-le-Pretre can provide a model for the rehabilitation of Europe's post-war housing stock. After the exhibition closed at the DAM, Mathias Böttger from the Deutsches Architekturzentrum in Berlin (DAZ) proposed that we bring the show to Berlin. The problem was that in the DAZ's Scharounsaal we were no longer confronted with the Ungers building. We felt that, in addition to the wallpaper panorama, we needed to design something for the inside of the room. Something Fantastic, the Berlin-based architecture firm, developed a system of walls for the space and hung the same solar curtains that Lacaton, Vassal, and Druot had installed in the Tour Bois-le-Pretre. In the Tour Bois-le-Pretre, the solar curtains help lower the heat loss between the inside and the outside and maintain a comfortable interior temperature without relying too much on mechanical systems. At the DAZ, however, the curtains acted as the exhibition's space dividers. Because we had more space the Scharounsaal, we could further emphasize the sensation of being inside an apartment of the Tour Bois-le-Pretre, even though there was no direct translation between the floor plans of the exhibition and those of Tour Bois-le-Pretre. It worked very well, and it was an interesting exercise in how to use a material in a different way and in a different context.

References

Lyotard J.-F. (1984), *The Postmodern Condition: A Report on Knowledge,* University of Minnesota Press, Minneapolis, pp. 71-82.

BRINGING THE SHOW CLOSE TO THE AUDIENCE

Andres Lepik

Architecture exhibitions struggle with the absence of real objects of desire; however, the contradiction between presenting the buildings that cannot be brought into the museum can also lead to a fruitful curatorial process. The dialogue between the exhibition and the space in which it is presented can become an architectural statement in and of itself. Alternatively, the exhibition can become an installation that reflects architectural concepts and that makes them tangible.

I think that the diffusion of programmes in curatorial studies generates two tendencies: on the one hand, the popularisation of the word, and on the other a more academic attempt to heighten, in terms of importance, the definition of curating (as has been done by *Log20* and *Oase 88*, the first magazines that have tried to bring together theory and history of architecture exhibitions). The surprising thing is that a process that has already happened in art, is happening much later in the architecture world. This is perhaps due to the fact that the curators of the most important architecture exhibitions have always been architects (let us only think about the curators of the Venice Biennale). I must confess that I am not an architect and that I feel very good about this. Architects dealing with architecture exhibitions often end up having conflicts of interest. I do not have these conflicts. I do not practice design and this makes me completely independent.

My career as a curator started with the exhibition of architectural models of the Renaissance. I worked first as a curatorial assistant in Berlin on the last venue of the show *Rinascimento. Da Brunelleschi a Michelangelo: La rappresentazione dell'architettura*. In Berlin we had the opportunity to present Antonio da Sangallo's model of St. Peter's in Rome in Schinkel's Rotunda in the Altes Museum. This became a stunning experience for everyone: Schinkel's classicism met with the sources of his inspiration.

In 1999 the MoMA in New York started preparing the

exhibition project *Mies in Berlin* and I contacted the chief curator, Terence Riley, to express my interest in bringing the exhibition to Berlin. The proposal was accepted and fortunately we were able to re-work the concept in some parts for the Altes Museum. We also managed to realise for the Rotunda a model of Mies' 1922 glass skyscraper project. It gave the visitors a strong impression of what would have happened if Mies had built it on Friedrichstraße. Later this model travelled to the third venue of the exhibition, that of the Caixa de Barcelona. Unfortunately, however, the amount of space available was inadequate for the model and in exhibiting terms the result looked extremely awkward. As a curator I feel challenged in thinking about the influence of objects on space and vice versa, and in reflecting on what the exhibition could look like within the space of its location.

In 2000, shortly before the Mies exhibition, I worked on an exhibition on Renzo Piano at the Neue Nationalgalerie, the last building designed by Mies van der Rohe. The space of the Neue Nationalgalerie is very challenging because of its vast openness, transparency and the absence of walls. A part of the preparatory work for the exhibition consisted in researching how this space had previously been used for architecture exhibitions in particular. One of the most fascinating projects to me was the museum's very first opening exhibition of 1968, which was dedicated to an exhibition on Mondrian and consisted of a presentation of panels hanging from the ceiling. I found this was an extremely beautiful installation as it referred directly to the transparency of the space. The idea for the exhibition might perhaps be directly tied to Mies himself because there was a similar installation in 1968. His 1958 Cullinan Hall (a museum extension he built in Houston, Texas), where he hung paintings directly from the ceiling, although without the supporting white panels that were used in the Berlin exhibition of 1968. In 1986 this idea of hanging panels from the ceiling was taken up again for a centennial exhibition on Mies that travelled from MoMA to Berlin. I found the idea of a completely weightless exhibition with objects floating around in it quite interesting. Another source of inspiration for the 1968 installation at the Neue Nationalgalerie may very

***Piet Mondrian*, inaugural exhibition, Neue Nationalgalerie, Berlin, 1968.**

Houston collectors, Cullinan Hall, Houston, 1968.

well have been one of the first architecture exhibitions to run in the Yale Art Gallery, designed by Louis Kahn, which used hanging tables suspended from the ceiling. This exhibition most likely dates back to 1953 or 1954, a long time before the exhibition with hanging paintings at the Cullinan Hall and also before the Mondrian exhibition at the Neue Nationalgalerie.

In regards to the Renzo Piano exhibition in the Neue Nationalgalerie in 2000, it was the architect's intent to use for this exhibition an itinerant exhibition of his work that he had already presented in Basel, at the Foundation Beyeler, as well as at other venues. It was an exhibition presented in a workshop-like form (as his office is called *Renzo Piano Building Workshop*), with exhibition material displayed on tables and with chairs scattered about for those who wanted to have a look at the sketch books reprinted for the exhibition. It had no relation whatsoever to the surrounding space since it was designed to be experienced in neutral rooms. I presented photographs of the previous spatial responses to the Neue Nationalgalerie to Renzo Piano and convinced him that he could not transfer an exhibition that had already been shown before, such as that of his itinerant exhibition, to this extremely challenging space. Renzo was immediately fascinated by the idea of hanging the exhibition and consequently changed the basic concept of his exhibition and designed hanging tables for the display. The show was a great success because the architecture of the exhibition was an expression of the exhibited architecture of Renzo Piano; it was a work in itself and it was the result of a curatorial process. The exhibition was a statement about the relation between the architecture of Renzo Piano and the architecture of Mies, which was hosting it.

In 2003 I worked with Rem Koolhaas on the *Content* exhibition. I knew about Koolhaas' long-time obsession with and adherence to Mies' work. At the same time I was aware of his strong disappointment with the official planning politics in Berlin, beginning in 1992 when he resigned from the jury for the Potsdamer Platz competition. In the first years of the new millennium he came regularly to Berlin as he was working on the designs of the Dutch embassy there. I asked him whether he was interested in doing a show in Mies' building. Koolhaas accepted and very soon presented his first conceptual sketch for the exhibition, which was a collage in the style of Mies. He kept repeating his motto *more is more* and wanted to present, in Berlin, AMO and OMA's ten years of production in the style of a *Polish flea market* – as he called it – placed within the gallery. His obsession with Mies resulted in destroying Mies' interior both ideologically and physically. In the collage that he presented we saw that he wanted to break some of the windows and extend the exhibition through the windows to containers placed on the platform around the building. Furthermore, he proposed to paint the black steel of the structure red. Fortunately, we were told there were not enough funds for the red paint and we also convinced him not to break the glass. Nevertheless, he did succeed in spraying the title of the exhibition on the glass façade of the building. The show was a great success, even in terms of experimenting with materials and display forms. Three trucks filled with models from his archives were unloaded over the course of several days. Since we did not have enough storage space, we decided to use the transportation crates as platforms for the exhibition. The process was intense and hard but it was a chance for Koolhaas to take his revenge on the aesthetics of Potsdamer Platz.

In 2007 when I started as a curator at the architecture and design department at MoMA in New York, I found the temporary exhibition space on the third floor far less exciting than the one at the Nationalgalerie.

The windows of the space are part of the original façade designed by Philip Johnson and saved by Yoshio Taniguchi when he did his extension. The rest of the space is not very interesting and you have to think carefully about what you can do with it. Picking a subject for my first exhibition was a major challenge. Nevertheless, I decided to somehow break the established rules of the exhibition programme in the architecture department.

***Modern Architecture. International exhibition*, MoMA, New York, 1932.**

I thought the strategy used by MoMA, beginning with the exhibition *Modern Architecture. International Exhibition* in 1932 and up until to the Deconstructivism exhibition in 1988, was mostly focused on promoting architecture in an elitist way. The architecture department was a kind

Deconstructivist Architecture,
MoMA, New York, 1988.

of star-making machine and for decades Philip Johnson kept it under his control so that the programme would not veer too far from his own ideas. Barry Bergdoll, who took Johnson's position following his death, and who also hired me as a curator, was the first chief curator to be free of this kind of dogmatic regime.
I thought that what was really missing in MoMA's architecture programme and design department was the issue of architecture's social relevance. I knew of some architects that had worked in this direction but I never thought of how to gather them together in a show.
So together with my team we started a global survey of what was happening at that moment, in 2008, which was a very important moment in the US because it was the height of the economic crisis. The exhibition I proposed to the exhibition committee received very positive reactions because everyone understood the relevance it had to the crisis. We called the exhibition *Small Scale Big Change – New Architectures of Social Engagement* and we presented eleven projects originating from Caracas to Bangladesh, from Burkina Faso to Rio de Janeiro, Johannesburg and Chile. The eleven projects focused on the problems of a global society in which two billion people were living in slums and informal housing. Such themes were not usual at MoMA and I wanted to keep the exhibition architecture of this show as simple as possible in order to respond to the low-budget spirit of most of the projects that were presented. I wanted to avoid criticism that might insist that too much money was being spent to build this exhibition and that it would be better invested in projects for communities in need. When I said to the exhibition department that I wanted to do the show just with chairs and tables on sawhorses, the carpenters smiled and asked me if I meant something like that of an IKEA display. I told them yes, that was the idea. So I had them build an IKEA type of display based on a simple and easy to understand layout. It was one of my main intentions to bring the show as close to the audience as possible and make it as simple as I could. I wanted to address MoMA's large audience, the public, about whose expectations for visiting the museum we know very little. Of course we know that they want to

see Picasso's *Demoiselles d'Avignon,* and that they want to take a break and perhaps have a coffee in the garden, but we do not know what they are specifically searching for besides the well-known highlights of the collection. Despite this fact, in observing visitors approach the architectural models, you can often hear them exclaim: "Wow! Architecture!" and watch them continue into the architecture gallery to look at the presentations; however, on their own they would have never decided to visit an architecture museum specifically. This is why I think it is important to create an attraction in the entrance of each exhibition that speaks to a large audience, and address more complex arguments later. The exhibition *Small Scale Big Change – New Architectures of Social Engagement,* for example, started with a scene from a film by Harun Farocki on brick making in Africa. People noticed the film without realizing it was about architecture and walked into the room. The process I used to allure them was that of showing very simple things and then making architecture's contribution to global society understandable. While you moved from project to project through the exhibition you were presented little by little with the exhibition's more complex messages. I attempted to orchestrate this idea through the space itself: first by means of the visual effect, then by gradually approaching the more complex matters. I realised I had succeeded when after the first tour I gave, which was addressed to the museum guards the day before the opening, resulted in these same guards coming to me afterwards to say that this had been the first show on architecture they had ever understood.

MoMA also has a tradition for 1:1 architecture exhibitions, starting in 1949 when Marcel Breuer built the first *House in the Garden.* More recently, in 2000, and still under the influence of Philip Johnson, MoMA created the *Young Architects Program* for the MoMA/PS1.

The programme consists of an annual competition for young architecture studios to realise a low cost installation. I was on the jury for three years and also curator for the Young Architects Program exhibition which presents all five competition entries. Each year the winning pavilion is built. The competition winners for the first year were the architects Dan Woods and Amale Andraos (WORK Architecture Company), former students of Rem Koolhaas, who made a great statement about urban farming and urban gardening with their project. The following year the winners were MOS (Michael Meredith and Hilary Sample), who built a kind of mammoth structure, a rather weird and hairy thing which showed me how exhibitions could become space themselves. Florian Idenburg's *Pole Dance,* presented in 2010, was an almost zero degree architecture represented by a sort of playground for adults. It was a three-month event aimed at letting visitors have fun, enjoy refreshments and barbecue in the enclosed garden of the PS1. *Pole Dance* exceeded our expectations in terms of visitor reception as people interacted with the poles, hanging from them and moving about on them and it turned into a kind of physically *healthy* and freeing installation. Most importantly, the YAP programme continued to give young architects in New York a chance to be noticed and published (we even did a small exhibition with all five competition entries which was discussed in the New York Times and led to a great deal of publicity for the winner). With similar installations, you can raise people's interest in architecture. *Pole Dance* developed into an exhibition for the general public as most visitors simply went to the garden to enjoy a beer and ended up seeing the installation and finding it interesting. The experience with the YAP programme taught me that architecture curators working on projects within a museum should step outside the box more often and really go out and work in the city or outside of the museum. This is exactly what I did last year in Munich due to the Pinakothek der Moderne being closed for six months for renovation. I was asked to think about a temporary structure that would solve the problem of not being able to visit the museum and view its content. The result was the temporary pavilion called *Schaustelle.* Designed by Jürgen Mayer H., it was intended to be built in Berlin, but was actually constructed in Munich. The programme of the four departments was successful. Hopefully this experience can show a possible way for future activities of the Architekturmuseum to be organised and exhibited outside of the building.

BEHIND THE GREEN DOOR
ARCHITECTURE AND THE DESIRE
FOR SUSTAINABILITY
curated by *ROTOR*

DogA OSLO 19 SEPTEMBER–1 DECEMBER 2013
DAC COPENHAGEN 7 FEBRUARY–9 JUNE 2014

Behind the Green Door, press conference in Brussels, 2013.

Behind the Green Door, setting up of the main exhibition in DogA Oslo, 2013.

Behind the Green Door, setting up of the main exhibition in DogA Oslo, 2013.

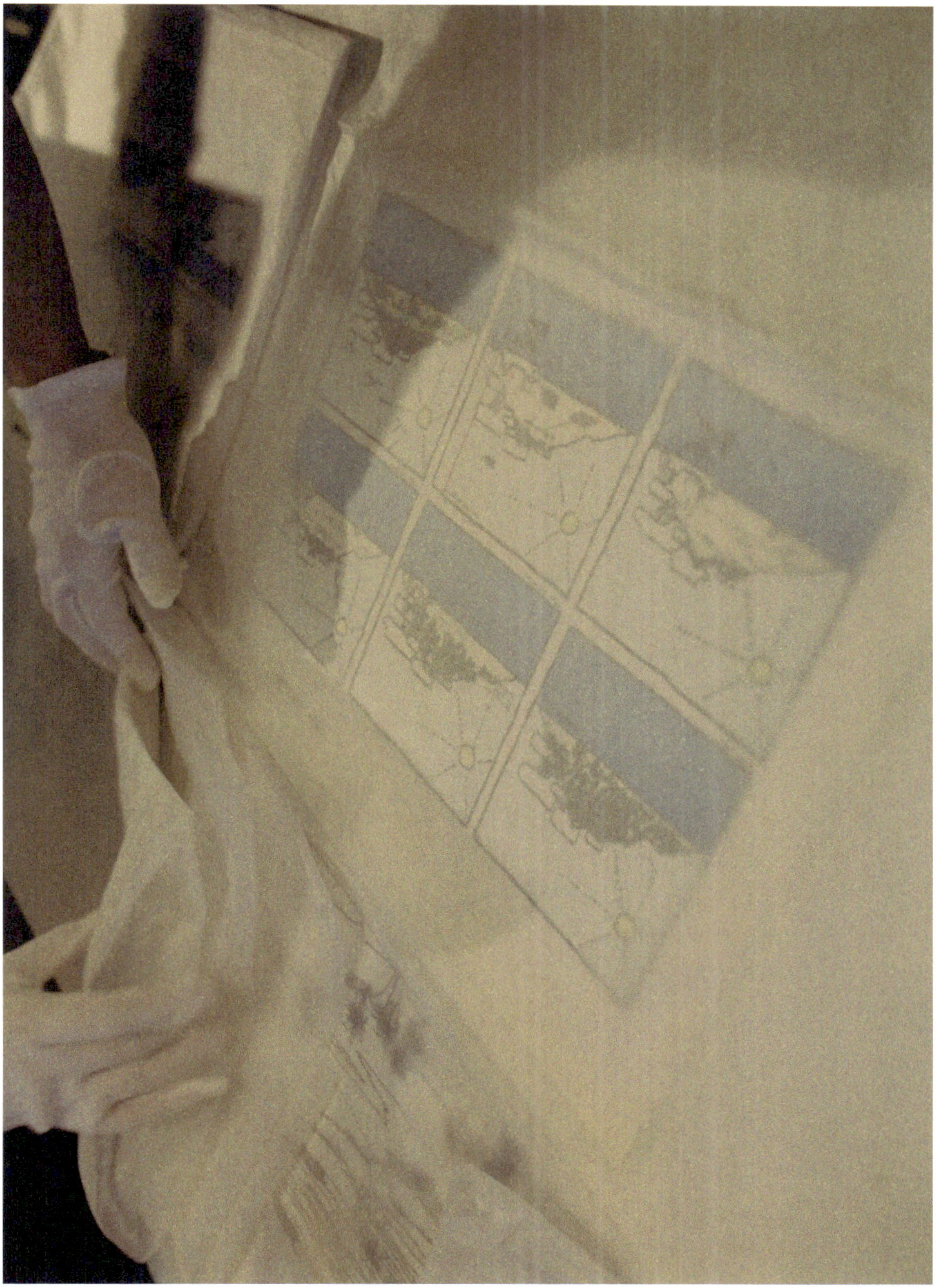

Behind the Green Door stories, with Eva Franch i Gilabert in DogA Oslo, 2013.

Behind the Green Door, view of the exhibition in DogA Oslo, 2013.

Behind the Green Door, view of the exhibition in DogA Oslo, 2013.

interview by
Roberto Gigliotti
recorded in Brussels
in May 2014

BEHIND THE GREEN DOOR ARCHITECTURE AND THE DESIRE FOR SUSTAINABILITY

Maarten Gielen — Rotor

First of all I would like to start with your personal opinion about displayed architecture. In the last years you curated and realised three popular architecture exhibitions: *Usus/Usures, OMA/Progress* and *Behind the Green Door*[1]. None of these exhibitions – for different reasons – could be defined a conventional show in terms of representation of the architecture and the built realm: *Usus/Usures* was the result of a research project on materials and materiality and tried to make visible the multiple meanings (without excluding the social or the political) attached to material wear and tear; *OMA/Progress* was an inside look into probably the most influential architecture office in the world; *Behind the Green Door* opened up a critical discussion around sustainability through the accumulation of a large amount of objects considered sustainable. In general how would you describe your attitude towards architecture exhibitions?

Our shows are indeed different from what one could call the stereotypical architecture exhibition. This usually consists of a presentation where each project is portrayed through a three-dimensional model, a plan and a description – it is a kind of *portfolio* show. Most of the time our intention is not to talk about architecture but to use architecture to talk about something else that is happening. Architecture is a field at the crossroads of

1 *Usus/Usures* (2010) was the Belgian contribution to the 12th International Architecture Exhibition of the Biennale di Venezia and is a project by Rotor in collaboration with Benedikte Zitouni and Ariane d'Hoop; *OMA/Progress* (2012) is a monographic exhibition on the work of OMA curated and designed by Rotor that took place in the Barbican Art Gallery in London; *Behind the Green Door – Architecture and the Desire for Sustainability* (2013) is the Oslo Architecture Triennale whose programme was curated by Rotor with a main exhibition at the DogA (Norwegian Centre for Design and Architecture).

many different disciplines. It is influenced by economy, by law, by taste, by aesthetic appreciation, by political ideas, etc. It is a discipline that can be used to talk almost about everything. What we did in the case of the Oslo exhibition is a good example: We looked at the architectural production of the last thirty years in order to talk about an evolution that is occurring in our society.
We used materials produced by architects as evidence to talk about something that is immaterial.

The position of curating the 2013 Oslo Architecture Triennale is the result of your winning an international competition together with the journal Criticat. What are the elements that enlivened your research while you worked out the proposal? What were your expectations and what were the relevant steps carried out between the concept you handed in and the realised exhibition?

This particular subject, sustainability, is something that we have been playing with implicitly in most of our projects over the last ten years. As we worked on the competition our first thought was about how the typical triennials normally work. Generally, curators suggest themes, which are as vague as possible. We wanted instead to focus the whole programme on one specific issue and from this approach raised our initial proposal. We asked that we be followed in this very precise subject and, since the goal was to be internationally relevant, we suggested the selection of a very small theme and let Oslo become the *capital* of that theme.
Furthermore we suggested that rather than splitting the budget in several small parts, we keep almost half of it for one single big show that would represent a central group of references which the other projects would refer to. We thought the main exhibition should work as a sort of backbone. In these two ways we completely perverted the brief of the competition because the budget had to be completely reconstructed and the theme we proposed was radically different from the one suggested (the Triennale had proposed something like *architectural quality in a*

booming economy, a very relevant but local question). We wanted to add a more internationally significant theme and find a way of dealing with it more locally. It was the jury, actually, that pointed out that the works of the Bruntland Commission had started in 1983, exactly thirty years before the 2013 Triennale. A further advantage for us was that we had never done projects in Northern Europe before. In some way the curatorship had always been committed to someone fairly local and so our being an outsider and the promise of connecting Oslo to an external network might have played to our advantage.

How did you let your research become an exhibition?

In the three cases you mention the process of conducting research and the process of doing the exhibition are the same. *Usus/Usures* was our first exhibition that belonged explicitly to the world of architecture and from there on we developed our practice so that decisions could be taken as late in the process as possible, even from within the exhibition space for instance. It might sound like just a detail but for the pedestals in the OMA exhibition in London we first bought a large amount of standard tables that we cut to the right height and size in the exhibition space, leaning them against the wall. This is a completely different approach from what you generally do with varnished plywood boxes that have to have exactly the right dimension to serve as pedestals. Such pedestals would need to be ordered weeks in advance in the exact number and size. It happens that we display models that we have never seen before and the only way to see them is to display them. Another example is that we love to print our captions in black and white on A4 sheets simply because this gives us the chance to make changes to them even at the very last moment. These sort of changes always happen during the mounting and this is the reason why we also try to do the mounting personally.

1:1 scale, in reference to models and architecture, is a recurring issue in the debate on architecture exhibitions.

According to the way you are describing your practice, one could almost say that you do not work with 1:1 models of the architecture displayed in the show, but rather with 1:1 models of the exhibition itself. You conceive the show and build it as a 1:1 model, which can then be inhabited by the displayed objects and by the visitor.

Yes, we could understand the way of physically working with these objects as the metaphorical value of the exhibition. The Oslo exhibition takes a clear position towards a series of other shows that we have seen in the last years where the curator comes up with a certain idea or certain notions related to sustainability and illustrates his/her point of view in an introductory wall text and explains it through so called *good examples*. We wanted to start explicitly from the idea that we do not know what sustainability is and we wanted to look at the question and offer to the visitor an exhibition which is an enquiry into everything that today is called sustainable by others. So we started looking at other exhibitions and going through architects' portfolios. When we came across the definition of sustainable, we identified something that could potentially be included in the exhibition. This way

2 It is my job to create universes, as the basis of one novel after another. And I have to build them in such a way that they do not fall apart two days later. Or at least that is what my editors hope. However, I will reveal a secret to you: I like to build universes which *do* fall apart. I like to see them come unglued, and I like to see how the characters in the novels cope with this problem. I have a secret love of chaos. There should be more of it. Do not believe – and I am dead serious when I say this – do not assume that order and stability are always good, in a society or in a universe. The old, the ossified, must always give way to new life and the birth of new things. Before the new things can be born the old must perish. This is a dangerous realization, because it tells us that we must eventually part with much of what is familiar to us. And that hurts. But that is part of the script of life. Unless we can psychologically accommodate change, we ourselves begin to die, inwardly. What I am saying is that objects, customs, habits, and ways of life must perish so that the authentic human being can live. And it is the authentic human being who matters most, the viable, elastic organism which can bounce back, absorb, and deal with the new.
Philip K. Dick, *How to build a universe that doesn't fall apart two days later,* 1978.

the show becomes rather the presentation of a question than the reinforcement of a point of view. We seldom use wall texts because we feel that often their words come across like the equivalent of *the voice of god:* you do not know who is talking; they make you think that they are absolutely true; they are so big that everybody has to see them. When we do need wall texts, we prefer to have two or three of them positioned in the exhibition space instead of one at the entrance. For instance, we did something similar in the *OMA/Progress* exhibition. One of the texts was a quote from a Philip K. Dick text[2] and the other one was actually hand written on the wall. Concerning the latter, we thought that this would reduce its impersonality. We wanted to make it slightly more fragile and, literally, we wrote the text one day before the opening of the exhibition.

And it was a questioning text …

The first part of the text contained a question in itself, almost saying: "Look, if you expect to see architecture in this exhibition you will be disappointed". The second half of the text marked our intention not to merely show architecture but to use the exhibition as a means to talk about the organisation of the world, about the constructed nature of everything that is around us, be it social codes, economic appreciation, etc.[3]

You were both curator and exhibition designer of the Oslo Architecture Triennale *Behind the Green Door;* this is not so extraordinary for an architecture exhibition, but rather unusual for other kinds of exhibitions. Can you contextu-

3 The problem with architecture exhibitions is that they can't show what they promise: architecture. When you can't put buildings or master plans in an exhibition space, you're condemned to some form of representation. That's where the trouble starts: do you show a complimentary photo of a summer's day when the building was brand new or do you show a picture of it on a rainy day twenty years later? Or do you show a model, a drawing, a video instead? Most of the time that choice depends on the architect – orchestrating your own work is part of the job.
This exhibition gives an outsider view on the inside of a particular office. *OMA/Pro-*

alise these two tasks that you simultaneously had to cope with? How did the two positions influence each other?

I think that in the same way that our exhibition projects are part of a research process, our built works and our designs are actually a kind of materialisation of our research projects. Just to give you an example,in our proposal for the interior of the new fashion and design centre MAD in Brussels (we handed in our competition proposal together with V+, another Brussels based office) we suggested to texturize all the walls in the building. The idea was to work on the building as a kind of a background, transforming our intervention into a sort of display like in an exhibition without content. Working with a very broad variety of materials, all white – expensive Carrara marble powder plaster, gypsum blocks, high gloss lacquered walls and matt textile walls – our project becomes an investigation into the neutrality of white. Without forgetting that in exhibitions the use of white is often the standard medium representing absence and silence, we wanted to test in how many ways we could pervert this white, to argue that it is not the neutrality of a material that defines the nature of what is in front of it. We organised that work as a research project and now we have an exhaustive material library for white materials, probably the biggest in Belgium (smile). Regarding our practice of exhibition making, we are very much used to working directly in the exhibition space. We often work with complex existing situations and have developed a set of tools for that. You could say that we are working on the idea of doing architecture in a way that puts design and execution very close together. You could call our projects 1:1 models in the same right.

***gress* is a portrait that consists mostly of found materials, materials that exist for reasons other than this exhibition. It shows architecture as a process, malleable to the specifics of each project. To shine light on why we've chosen the objects we show, each exhibit is accompanied by a caption on the floor. We've given the last word to OMA, the handwritten comments are theirs. Don't let all of this explanation distract you. This show is still about the essence of architecture: how do you want the world to be? What changes is the absence of rhetoric; we invite you to think for yourself. Rotor, 4 October 2011.**

In a way this approach is similar to what we do when we open the cases of the objects to be presented in an exhibition. We consider the situation in which we find ourselves and how we can play with the meaning of all these objects. We take one piece and put it next to another one and this becomes a statement; because it would be different if we presented it isolated, maybe with a white backdrop glorifying it. Furthermore, to glorify a forgotten object has a completely different meaning than to glorify an icon. I do not have the skills to understand all this on paper; when you are in a space, you have a feeling for it, whether it is an office space or something else. You feel what you can or cannot do and then you try out things and see what happens.

Does this mean that for your exhibitions you could not imagine another possibility other than being both curator and designer?

I could imagine designing a scenography for some institutions whose work we appreciate, such as the CCA in Montréal to name but one. There are many people we could work with; it is not an ego thing. Still, if we take responsibility of an exhibition, we want to control it (although I do not like to use this word, I think that in this case it is the right one). If you accept the idea that a neutral language cannot exist in an exhibition, then you cannot delegate, you have to follow this language. On the other hand, it does not mean that in our team everybody is doing the same job. With certain projects some of us have the task of being scenographers, while the others concentrate on the curating. This is for example the way we dealt with the Oslo exhibition: while Lionel Devlieger and I were busy with the research work, Benjamin Lassere and Tristan Boniver where more involved in the scenography.

How much does your open attitude, which distances itself on purpose from any *a priori* positioning, only generate questions without offering any answers? One might expect from you a clearer statement… Do you have an answer or do you firmly refuse this kind of position? If indeed the latter is true, how then does this attitude reflect itself in the form of the exhibition?

When we argue that we refuse to take a clear position or that we try to keep an open point of view inside the exhibition space, this is often a provocation, a trick, because the exhibition in itself and the way it is organised is already a statement in itself. The Belgian Pavilion at the Venice Biennale in 2010 showed used building parts, hardly a neutral thing to do at the Biennale. And in Oslo it was a statement to delegate to others the search for a common understanding of sustainability. Our assertion was that there is no absolute form of sustainability and in a context where the debate is dominated by positivists that claim the opposite, this is also quite a statement. The idea to present the objects as tools for a discussion that would take place within our framing of such objects was not gratuitous and we showed that there are many subtle ways to frame the discussion that we wanted to generate.

But the frame within which this discussion can happen is spatial. From a cultural point of view, the position you take in the organisation of *Behind the Green Door* is very clear. Thirty years after the Bruntland Commission you want to open a discussion on the issue of sustainability while trying to avoid positions that might be taken for granted, and to explore the meaning of the term sustainability in a moment in which this term almost seems to lose its importance due to it being so thoroughly overused (and abused). Even if you apparently conceive the show more as a *discursive* space than a *contemplative* one, you spatially organise the 600 objects you selected in a very clear way. The visitor can feel spatial and visual connections, although the bulk of objects might be overwhelming or disorientating. How important is the encounter between the visitor and the objects? Do the displayed objects really have the capacity of bringing the issue nearer to a broad public?

For the Oslo Triennale we had a 1:10 model, which we tried to use in order to establish these visual connections, but in many cases we had to adapt our project during the construction because the objects happened not to be exactly how we had expected. Think about any object in front of you right now: you have an idea of it but then you put it in front of a background and you start seeing details like, for example, traces of wear on its surface and so on, and the object is not itself anymore. You have to be very sensitive to this. I am still not sure how this happens and I think that we often implicitly refer to some code that people know. In Venice the space of the Belgian Pavilion literally asked for a formal display that was very close to the way you would normally exhibit paintings. In Oslo we started from a warehouse and this is a completely different context. The exhibition changed a lot between Oslo and Copenhagen[4] because in Denmark we exhibited in a sort of white cube. Even if it has wooden floors and wooden columns the Danish Architecture Centre has white walls, which changed the perception a lot. In Oslo we implicitly referred to the format of the natural history museum or of the cabinet of curiosities and this influenced our very dense form of displaying, which further led to the conception of the captioning device that was structured in relationship to the displayed objects.
In every exhibition we did, we paid attention not to put anything superfluous in the show and we avoided anything that could seem to be there just because it was pretty or because everybody would have easy and quick access to it. We feel a commitment towards the audience. Of course, budgets always define a project, but even more so is it the attention that you can expect from the

4 *Behind the Green Door* was exhibited in Oslo, at the DogA, between the 13th of September and the 1st of December 2013 and moved then to Copenhagen, where it was exhibited at the DAC (Danish Architecture Centre) from the 6th of February to the 8th of June 2014.

audience that makes the difference. In Venice we could expect the average visitor to pay approximately forty seconds of attention to our pavilion and we took this as a brief: this was the amount of time we had to work with in order to say something. For the Oslo exhibition we could count with a time lapse between twenty minutes and an hour. Oslo is a fairly small city: people who went to Oslo to see *Behind the Green Door* had time for us. We learned a lot about this issue of visitor attention for an exhibition during the OMA show. We realised the OMA show was perhaps too dense and did not give enough guidance. This made it very interesting for architects but perhaps too complicated for a larger audience. That is why we came up with the idea of prominently using guided tours as a means of activating the Oslo exhibition: two guided tours given by an expert every week. Basically, an expert meant for us someone with a deep knowledge of one of the subjects related to the show: it could be a specialised engineer or a sociologist, but even a patient could be considered an expert on the life in a hospital, in a way. Each expert chose ten objects and used them to give a very subjective reading of the exhibition. In a sense this experiment allowed us to have a different exhibition twice a week. Each time the exhibition changed because each guide sequenced the pieces differently and the visitors criss-crossed the space according to a different path. By creating different sequences you create different meanings and this is the way we create access into the content of the exhibition.

The exhibition is discussed on numerous occasions and in various forms: during a series of organised talks on the subject, in a book published along with the exhibition, and in the exhaustive catalogue following the exhibition. Real objects meet invented stories contained in the first publication… can you describe what different results arise from conveying content through visual arrangements compared to conveying content through other means such as texts?

Leuven, 2012, Artefact Festival, STUK Leuven, 2013.

Grindbakken, installation view, 2012.

Exhibitions are efficient because they create an actuality; they are places and possess the ability to involve many people. If we had done only a book we would have probably got in contact only with the architects and with the offices that we exhibited. For the Oslo Triennale, instead, the books are *complementary* to the exhibition. We wanted to have two publications that would accompany the show from the very onset. These were to represent an aspect of the work that was not designed for the presentation of results but for setting the terms of the debate. For the first one we thought about a newspaper or paperback, something cheap. Whilst the real book should come after the exhibition. We decided to include one serious text, which is *Pockets of Sustainability*[5], in the first publication and then we wanted to introduce a humorous part on the subject. We wanted to fix stereotypes in order to work against them. In the same way that we need the abstract idea of a prototypical architecture exhibition, which actually does not exist, we wanted a prototypical idea of what a climate engineer or a lobbyist is. Therefore we listed and described fictional characters and collected them in the *Who is who of sustainability*[6] section of the book, which you could buy at the entrance of the exhibition.

In an exhibition you can look at many objects in many different ways; their meaning depends on what you write in the caption. For example, there was a Playmobil toy in the exhibition. If you were to put it in a different exhibition, it could be a piece of innovation in plastic production technology, or it might be a piece about the act of playing, or it could be anything we choose it to talk about. We framed the object very clearly and removed some of its meanings. We removed the possibility of playing with it, and we even dramatized it in the way we displayed it, and although it is a cheap object, we used a glass cover to give it some *grandeur,* to let the observer think of it as something very precious. The pedestal,

5 Gielen M., in collaboration with Devlieger L. (2013), Pockets of Sustainability, in *Behind the Green Door, Architecture and the Desire of Sustainability,* Oslo Architecture Triennale, pp. 23-32.

6 Devlieger, L./ROTOR, *Who's Who in Green Building,* ibid. pp. 33-48.

the bonnet, the lighting, the disposition of the object, the fact that it was raised above all the other exhibits produced the meaning of that object.
But the use of originals is not the only strategy we use. In *Leuven, 2012*,[7] an exhibition that we consider as the preliminary research for the Oslo Triennale, we looked at everyday scenes taking place in the territory of Leuven, a Belgian city that in the future wants to become carbon neutral and that could therefore be branded as sustainable. We explicitly did not want to work with photographs because they would have been too literal. Instead we wanted to use a form of representation that people could accept as close to some form of reality without being realistic. We commissioned Robert Suermondt to produce paintings in which faces are blurred, certain details left white because irrelevant to the scene, and the context made to look faded or blurred. We used these elements in the same way that we put the Playmobil toy under glass.
In *Grindbakken*,[8] we were asked to install an exhibition in a disused gravel and sand bunker, a concrete space that was about to be painted white. Instead of bringing objects into a white cube, we defined areas that should not be painted in order to highlight certain things like, for example, a little plant that grows between rocks and is often seen on boardwalks and façades and for this reason has always been persecuted by pesticides administered in the name of public good. Only in recent times, since this plant grows very well on rock surfaces, has it been discovered to be the ideal plant for green roofs; so now you can even get government funding if you plant it. It is the story of a villain becoming a hero, something like a bandit becoming a champion. It is one of the best things we have done so far because it shows that things can change, it shows that to be a villain or not is not contained in the subject but is constructed by a common understanding, it is a social construction and it is something that can change.
I do not think that we have any fetish for originals.

7 *Leuven, 2012* Artefact Festival, STUK Leuven, February 2013.
8 Grindbakken, Gent, September–October 2012.

For us the starting point for the Oslo exhibition was an image we had in mind of a little guy coming from Mars to Earth and trying to make sense out of things by collecting artefacts. A bit like a colonist would do in an African village when collecting all the spoons and totems and all those kind of things that have a certain *aura*. The big print hanging on the background of the exhibition space tells exactly this story: it is as if we were looking at the earth (or at what happens on the earth) from a distance. It is almost as if the exhibition space were on the moon and from there we were looking at the earth from a distance. We are not in the same space as our planet, the thinking is separated from the acting, the space of the exhibition is disconnected from the practice.

EXHIBITIONIST UTTERANCES

Tina di Carlo

This text is the transcription of the talk given by Tina di Carlo in Bolzano during the conference Displayed Spaces. New means of architecture presentation through exhibitions *that represents the starting point for this publication.*

This talk proposes to open the discursive space of the exhibition and of the conference by invoking the 1988 *Deconstructivist Architecture* exhibition at the Museum of Modern Art, New York, as a precedent. The exhibition ran from 23 June–30 August 1988 and was organised by Philip Johnson with the assistance of Mark Wigley. It included three galleries, with ten projects from the previous decade by the following seven architects: Coop Himmelblau, Peter Eisenman, Frank O. Gehry, Zaha M. Hadid, Rem Koolhaas, Daniel Libeskind and Bernard Tschumi. While many are familiar with the catalogue cover – a yellow and orange-coloured "[d]etail of a project by Coop Himmelblau, transmitted by fax" (Johnson, Wigley, 1988) – few actually remember the show.[1]

The installation was arguably small, if not incidental. The first gallery was dedicated to a selection of works from the Russian avant-garde, including works by "El Lissitzky, Kasimir Malevich, Liubov Popova, Alexander Rodchenko, Vladimir Tatlin, and others."[2] The second and third galleries featured the following: Parc de la Villette, Paris, 1982 by Tschumi; City Edge Competition, Berlin, 1987 by Libeskind; Familian Residence and Gehry House, Santa Monica, 1987 by Gehry; Biology Center for the University of Frankfurt, 1987 by Eisenman; The Peak, Hong Kong, 1982 by Hadid; Rooftop Remodeling, Vienna,

1 In January 2013, Barry Bergdoll, then the Philip Johnson Chief Curator of Architecture and Design, mounted a small retrospective of the show in the Painting and Sculpture galleries. This was accompanied by a symposium at Columbia and MoMA that included Bergdoll, Mark Wigley, Peter Eisenman and Bernard Tschumi.

2 Museum of Modern Art Press Release: *Deconstructivist Architecture, June 23–August 30, 1988,* June 1988, p. 1. Exhibition 1489, Museum of Modern Art Archives, New York. p. 2.

1985, Hamburg Skyline, 1986 and Apartment Building, Vienna, 1986 by Coop Himmelblau; Rotterdam Building and Tower, 1982 by Rem Koolhaas. Given the polemics and controversy that surrounded the show – it received five times as much press as any other architecture exhibition of similar size – at issue is the constitutive role of language within the apparatus of the exhibition.

The contribution of language in the creation of value

I would like to begin by opening a question about the economy of language: in particular, to consider how the circulation of language enters into exhibitionist practices and how language contributes to the creation of value through its circulation. How does it enter into the discursive space of architecture and into the canonical effects of exhibitions? In short how do language and text construct the apparatus of the exhibition, and how, in turn, does the exhibition construct them? Within architecture I would also suggest that this is an inherently spatial issue, or question, of how the space of the exhibition – and thus of architecture – and that of language are co-constitutive. In the case of the *Deconstructivist Architecture* exhibition this is particularly pertinent because the early theoretical position as established by Wigley in the relation of deconstruction to architecture – a relation subsequently lost in the stylisation of the show – was one of discourse.

Language enters into the circulation of architecture

On my way to Gatwick Airport I saw an advert about the city of London that said: "You love London. So do we. Discover and do more with our curated list of events." Curating it seems has entered into common parlance, informing how to orchestrate everything from planning our visits to cities, to choosing our menus. One could argue that this sort of mainstream – the currency that curating has assumed within culture, even within language – is indicative of a certain economy.

In the last years, we have seen an increase currency in the discussion about curating architecture and exhibitions in general. The journals *Log 20: Curating Architecture,* published in fall 2010, for which I was the consulting editor and *OASE 88: Exhibition. Showing and Producing Architecture,* edited by Veronique Patteeuw, Tom Vandeputte and Cristophe Van Gerrewy in 2012 stand as only a few cases in point. Witness as well the plethora of biennales. But the question then is whether this currency adds value or rather *de-values?*

It could be said that, contrary to the intended objective of the proliferation of exhibitions and biennials, to the rise of curatorial practices over the last ten to fifteen years, and to the entry of the word *curating* into the everyday, this currency contributes if not to the devaluation of architecture, to the devaluation of architects. While architecture attains currency through circulation on the one hand, this currency renders it not only commonplace within an overly saturated market but increases an atmosphere in which we as curators and architects are continually devalued, both financially and ideologically.

Language as gossip

Within an exhibition, language as a form of media enters into the circulation of architecture – via wall texts, wall labels, press releases and press reviews, catalogue essays –, it enters the museum itself, department stores, it enters on-site, at expositions, on Facebook, Twitter, Pinterest, Instagram. Language enters as one medium or media among others. Certainly as it became evident in the 1988 *Deconstructivist Architecture* exhibition, and perhaps even more forcefully, as Beatriz Colomina has suggested early on in *Privacy and Publicity* (1996). Yet perhaps now as Twitter proves all too well, language enters as a form of gossip in the construction of architecture and the exhibition, as a construction of social, political relations. People begin to talk. Relations are created.

Catherine Ingraham wrote at the time of the *Deconstructivist Architecture* exhibition that the “hype and hysteria” surrounding the exhibition resulted in “the proliferation of embarrassing references to ‘deconstructivism’ in every fashion magazine, cocktail party, and trendy gathering in the American world” (1988). Michael

Sorkin launched a scathing review in the *Village Voice* in December 1987 that predated the exhibition by almost nine months, launching it into public attention. At issue was not architecture *per se,* but the ethics of Johnson's perceived antics. Yet it was this review that garnered interest. How then an exhibition, and also architecture, constitutes language, and language – or perhaps better said *the talk* constitutes the exhibition and its canonical effect – must be questioned. How is an exhibition written in and through language, and its discursive space opened through the (spoken) utterance?

Exhibitions, and those that surround them – the stakeholders – give people something to talk about. Moreover, when we look back, what remains is not the exhibition as a visual construct but, I would suggest, the exhibition as text, as it is written in and through language and text–the catalogue, the exhibition's reviews, press releases, archival material–and as a discursive construction of the institutional apparatus.

Media as propaganda?

> *Dear Mrs. Sullivan:*
>
> *I hope that the topics which I have listed below will be helpful to you in the discussion at the dinner at Mrs. Crane's on April 14.*
>
> *1. Exhibitions should have a definite purpose.*
>
> *I believe every show should have a point. The American Show is lacking in this particular. An exhibition planned with the idea of explaining and developing a certain problem or aspect of modern art is much more certain to attract the public.*
>
> *2. Wider range of the arts.*
>
> *The exhibition should include other branches of the arts such as photography, architecture, etc.*
>
> *3. Extension of education.*
>
> *I am certainly in favor of a more extensive program of lectures although I realize that there are certain difficulties to be encountered to realize this in actual practice.*
>
> *4. Museum publications.*
>
> *There should be more publications of the Museum, especially monographs on the various phases of modern art.*

5. Library.
Certainly the library should have a more complete photographic collection and should be equipped with more books on every related subject.
6. Advertising.
I believe a discussion of dignified ways in which the Museum might attract attention to itself would bring out many interesting suggestions. Such details as placards at the entrance, various types of leaflets explaining the work of the Museum, calling attention to future exhibits, even a placard in the elevator might lead to definite results [...][3]

In this letter to Mrs. Sullivan, dated 1931, Philip Johnson outlines the importance of publicity and programming in the development of an exhibition. The letter pre-dates the 1932 *Modern Architecture: International Exhibition.* Already here the apparatus of the exhibition that includes programming, education, and lectures becomes apparent. In short Johnson lays out the exhibitionist practices that he will employ throughout his career, in which the emphasis is on publicity, what he, at the time, calls advertising but which, in essence, each of the constituent elements would comprise.

"Exhibitions should have a point," Johnson states. And part of this point, I would argue, was to create a stir. As Herbert Muschamp noted in 1988, Johnson long ago knew he could get more mileage out of being bad than being good. He was also unabashed about capitalising on the media.

In an interview with Patricia C. Phillipps for example, he describes the *International Style* for which, he said, Hitchcock codified, Barr conceived and he did the "propaganda and the screaming." Of the controversy and polemics that surrounded *Deconstructivist Architecture,* he told Philips "[I]t would bring attention to architecture" (Filler, 1988 and Phillips, 1988).

The exhibition, as such, becomes not just a chronicle of architecture, or a mechanism involved in its production, in experimentation, and in the production

3 Philip Johnson, letter to Mrs. Cornelius J. Sullivan, March 27, 1931. Exhibition 15, Museum of Modern Art Archives, New York.

of knowledge but it adds to its currency. It begins to perpetuate a greater public recognition of architecture, of its role within culture, through talk – in this case the polemics and debate surrounding it that, as said before, have as much to do with Johnson's antics as with the questionable term itself.

Polemics and debate

It could be argued then that the installation of the 1988 *Deconstructivist Architecture* exhibition was incidental to its effect. Furthermore, it could also be said that what constituted the exhibition *per se* was the press and polemics that surrounded it, which entered into the popular and architectural discourse as early as December 1987. And finally, it could be argued that the polemics that surrounded the show came down to two pivotal factors: the title and Johnson himself.

In short the debate came down to language – the naming of an –ism or –ist, "titled arcs and warped planes" that violated the pure space of the museum's modernity – and to the gossip that surrounded Johnson. The distillation of an aesthetic style or movement recalled the intellectual origins of the museum, as established by founding director Alfred H. Barr, Jr., as well as the distillation of a social imperative to style, within the *International Style* as codified by MoMA. Johnson's antics, regarding ethics and architecture, fuelled the debate, as did the divergent positions of Wigley and Johnson.

Was *Deconstructivist Architecture* a reference to the literary movement of deconstruction as theorised by Jacques Derrida?

What, if any, relation did it have to Constructivism?

Was the exhibition a "nihilistic stunt", as Hilton Kramer claimed (1988) or a "Decon Job", as Michael Sorkin wrote (1987), when he – in the words of Muschamp – "first went public with the shorty" (1988).

Was it Johnson's idea or not? Or was it, as

Stanley Tigerman and others would claim, the idea of Paul Florian and Stephen Wierzbowksi, and presented to Johnson by Aaron Betsky in a meeting in October 1987 in the form of "Violated Perfection"?[4]

Was the title of the exhibition *Deconstructivist Architecture* the "lexical alchemy" of Joseph Giovannini (1990), who publically claimed and was credited for its invention, even years after the exhibition's close?

Did it coin a new movement, a new style, despite the curator's protests to the contrary and particularly given the speculated symmetry to the *International Style* (Gandee, 1990)?

What of the divergent positions of the architects themselves?

And how were the seven architects selected? Was it a members only meeting at the Century Club, as Sorkin suggests (op. Cit.)? Who was in or who was out...?

Language constitutes exhibition/exhibition constitutes language

In summary *Deconstructivist Architecture* was a local New York phenomenon. Polemics fuelled the press. Reception in the press fuelled the effect. The exhibition received five times as much press as the other exhibition in the series of which it was a part, and twice as much as any previous exhibition of comparable size. It was in the press for over a year. The polemics and debate was due as much to Johnson's personal politics and antics as to the theoretical issues surrounding the show. Even before it opened, *Deconstructivist Architecture* was heralded as the end to postmodernism, making its prophetic effect, self-fulfilling.

So it raises the question of not only how language constitutes the exhibition, and how the exhibition, in turn, constitutes language, but how each construct

4 February 26, 1988 letter to Stuart Wrede, received 3/8/88, Stanley Tigerman FAIA

architecture. How can language influence the production and canonization of architecture, forcing it to change directions? How can we use language and its circulation as text not just as a way to structurally model architecture or architecture exhibitions, but also to open a discursive space for architecture and exhibitions?
When language becomes currency that influences value it is not – as I suggest – only a discursive question, but an ethical one as well.

References

Colomina B. (1996), *Privacy and Publicity: Modern Architecture as Mass Media,* MIT Press.

Filler M. (1988), *Philip Johnson: Deconstruction Worker,* interview, May.

Gandee C. (1988). The Revolution of '88?: Postmodernism is passé according to an upcoming exhibition at MOMA, *House & Garden,* May, v.160, no. 5, p.37.

Giovannini J. (1990), On Deconstructivism, letter to the Home Section, Home & Garden, *The New York Times,* 7 June.

Ingraham C. (1988), Milking Architecture or Cow was the Show, *Inland Architect,* v. 32, no. 5, p. 62.

Johnson P., Wigley M. (1988), *Deconstructivist Architecture,* New York: Museum of Modern Art, p. 4.

Kramer H. (1988), Twerpy MOMA Architecture Show. Another Nihilist Stunt by Johnson, *The New York Observer,* 4–11 July.

Muschamp H. (1988), Ground Up, *Artforum,* April.

Phillips P. C. (1988), The Greatest Show Unearthed, *Stroll,* 1 June.

Sorkin M. (1987), Cannon Fodder, *Village Voice,* December.

Giovanna Borasi

Giovanna Borasi is an architect, curator and editor. She has developed several research projects, with a particular focus on how environmental and social issues are influencing today's urbanism and architecture. She has been editor of *Lotus International* (1998–2004) and deputy editor in chief of *Abitare* (2012-2013). Since January 2014, she is chief curator at the Canadian Centre for Architecture, Montréal where she worked previously as Curator of Contemporary Architecture (2005–2013).

Emanuela De Cecco

Emanuela De Cecco is an art critic and associate professor of Contemporary Art History, at the Faculty of Design and Art of the Free University of Bozen Bolzano. Among the her most relevant publications: in 2000 she edited with Gianni Romano the volume *Contemporanee,* Costa & Nolan, Milan; in 2002 *Zingonia: Art, integration, multiculture,* A & M Bookstore, Milan; in 2004 *Tacita Dean,* Postmedia, Milan; in 2010 *Arte-mondo. Storia dell'arte, storie dell'arte,* Postmedia, Milan; in 2012 *Anna Valeria Borsari. Due quadri, le cornici, il muro e altre questioni,* Postmedia, Milan and *Luca Vitone: Acting places,* Museion, Bolzano. Her most recent text *Notes on Electric Blue: movements of body and soul,* is part of the catalogue of the Exhibition *Adrian Paci, Vies en Transit,* Jeu de Paume, Paris, 2013.

Tina Di Carlo

Tina di Carlo, a former curator of architecture and design at the Museum of Modern Art, New York, is a Ph.D. fellow in Exhibiting Architecture: Placement and Displacement, funded by the Norwegian Research Council at the Oslo Centre for Critical Architectural Studies. She holds a Masters in Architecture from Harvard University and advanced degrees in Art History and Visual Cultures from the Courtauld Institute, London and Goldsmiths, respectively. She was the contributing editor of *Log 20: Curating Architecture* and is the author of the forthcoming *Exhibitionism* (Sternberg Press) funded by the Graham Institute for Advanced Studies in the Fine Arts.

Kersten Geers

Kersten Geers studied at the University of Ghent and at the Esquela Tecnica Superior de Arquitectura in Madrid, Spain. He worked in Rotterdam for Maxwan/Max.1 Architects until 2001 and from 2001 to 2005 for Neutelings Riedijk Architects. He was a tutor at the TU Delft, the University of Ghent and the Accademia di Architettura di Mendrisio, and a guest lecturer and guest critic for the Berlage Institute in Rotterdam, and for Columbia University in New York, among other institutions. He currently is associate professor at EPFL, Lausanne. He is founding member and editor of *San Rocco* magazine, and frequently publishes essays on architecture in a variety of magazines and books. In 2002 he founded Office Kersten Geers David Van Severen together with David Van Severen. In 2008 they were awarded with the Belgian Prize for Architecture and in 2010 with the Silver Lion at the 12th Venice Biennial of Architecture.

Maarten Gielen

Maarten Gielen is a designer, manager, and researcher of the Brussels-based collective Rotor, comprised of people sharing a common interest in material flows in industry and construction. On a practical level, Rotor handles the conception and realization of design and architectural projects. On a theoretical level, Rotor develops critical positions on design, material resources, and waste through research, exhibitions, writings, and conferences. The group recently curated *OMA/Progress,* a large exhibition on the work of OMA, at the Barbican in London. Together with Lionel Devlieger, Gielen was curator of the 2013 Oslo Architecture Triennale titled *Behind the Green Door – architecture and the desire for sustainability.*

Anne Holtrop

Anne Holtrop is an independent architect based in Amsterdam. His work ranges from models to temporary spaces and buildings on which he occasionally collaborates with the artists Krijn de Koning and Bas Princen. He is course director of the master Studio for Immediate Spaces at the Sandberg Instituut Amsterdam, and was editor of *OASE,* an architectural journal for architecture, from 2005 till 2013. For his practice he has has been awarded several grants from the Fonds BKVB, as well as receiving the Charlotte Köhler Prize for Architecture from the Prince Bernhard Cultural Foundation.

Wilfried Kuehn

Wilfried Kuehn holds a degree in architecture from the Milan Polytechnic and is partner in the architectural firm Kuehn Malvezzi in Berlin. From 2006 to 2012 he was professor for exhibition design and curatorial practice at the Karlsruhe University for Arts and Design / ZKM where he founded *Displayer,* a periodical focussing on curatorial design and exhibition making. In 2011 he curated the exhibition *Carlo Mollino. Maniera Moderna* together with Armin Linke at Haus der Kunst, Munich, in 2014 he curated *Hollein* at MAK Vienna. With Kuehn Malvezzi he earned a reputation in the field of museum and exhibition design, starting with the spaces of the *Documenta 11* exhibition venues for Okwui Enwezor in 2002, followed by the extension of the *Hamburger Bahnhof Museum der Gegenwart* in Berlin for the *Friedrich Christian Flick Collection* in 2004. Since then Kuehn Malvezzi have completed the *Julia Stoschek Collection* in Düsseldorf, the extension and museography of the *Museum Belvedere* in Vienna, the rehabilitation of the *Museum Berggruen* and the *Kunstgewerbemuseum* in Berlin as well as the spaces of the *Staedel Museum,* the *Liebieghaus* and the *MMK 2* in Frankfurt.

Andres Lepik

Andres Lepik studied history of art and German philology at the Universities of Augsburg and Munich and worked on his dissertation on Renaissance architectural models at the Bibliotheca Hertziana in Rome. He was a curator at the Staatlichen Museen in Berlin in 1994. From 2004 to 2007 he took the direction of the 20th and 21st Century

Architecture Collection of the Kunstbibliothek. From 2007 to 2011 he worked as curator at the Department for Architecture and Design of the Museum of Modern Art, New York. In 2011-2012 he was the Loeb-Fellow at the Graduate School of Design, Harvard University. Since October 2012 he is professor of History of Architecture and Curatorial Practices at the TU-München and director of the Architekturmuseum at the Pinakothek der Moderne. Andres Lepik has curated numerous architecture exhibitions, including: *Architekturmodelle der Renaissance: die Harmonie des Bauens von Alberti bis Michelangelo* (Altes Museum, 1995); *Renzo Piano. Architekturen des Lebens* (Neue Nationalgalerie, 2000); *Mies in Berlin* (Altes Museum, 2001); *Content. Rem Koolhaas und OMA/AMO Bauten, Projekte und Konzepte seit 1996* (Neue Nationalgalerie 2003/2004). At the Museum of Modern Art he curated *Small Scale, Big Change. New Architectures of Social Engagement* (2010/2011) and in Munich *AFRITECTURE, Building Social Change* (2013/14), *Show & Tell – Architekturgeschichte(n) aus der Sammlung* (2014), *The Good Cause: Architecture of Peace – Divided Cities* (2014), *Lina Bo Bardi 100* (2014).

Ilka & Andreas Ruby

Trained as an architect and an architecture historian, respectively, Ilka Ruby and Andreas Ruby are the founding partners of textbild, an office that authors and edits books, magazines, and essays, curates exhibitions and conferences, and consults architects and institutions. In 2008, they founded their own publishing house, Ruby Press for books on architecture, art and other spatial practices. They have curated a number of architectural exhibitions; most recently they co-curated the Montenegro Pavilion at the 14th Architectural Biennial of Venice.

Something Fantastic

Something Fantastic is a Berlin-based office engaged with architecture, the city, sustainability and design. It was founded in 2010 by Elena Schütz, Julian Schubert and Leonard Streich (all Dipl. Ing. Arch UdK Berlin). Their claim that architecture and urbanism affects everything, and vice versa is affected by everything, results in an inter-national and pan-disciplinary practice. In order to achieve a more beautiful, equal, comfortable, and pleasurable environment for everyone, anywhere and anytime, Something Fantastic writes, lectures, teaches, curates, plans and designs in various scales and media. Something Fantastic's work has been exhibited at the Venice Biennale 2012 and 2014, the Sao Paulo Biennal 2013, and Haus der Kulturen Welt Berlin, and has been been published in magazines like *Domus*, or *Horizonte*, and in books like e.g. *Re-Inventing Construction* or *What is Critical Spatial Pratice?* After teaching at UdK Berlin, École Nationale Supérieur de Architecture Paris-Malaquais, ETH Zurich, RWTH Aachen and HfG Karlsruhe, the partners are currently directing the Master of Advanced Studies in Urban Design at ETH Zurich, focusing on informal settlements and mass housing in Brazil.

Roberto Gigliotti

Roberto Gigliotti graduated in architecture from the IUAV in Venice and in landscape architecture from the Edinburgh College of Art. He is associate professor of Interior and Exhibit Design at the Faculty of Design and Art of the Free University of Bozen Bolzano. His main research interests include the exhibition of architecture and the contemporary urban public space. He is founding member of Lungomare Bolzano and vice-president of ar/ge kunst Galerie Museum, Bolzano. His publications include *Traum Stadt Wir* (co-edited in 2005 with Angelika Burtscher and Manuela Demattio) and *Casa Tabarelli 1968–2008*.

Eva Mair

Eva Mair is an architect educated in Graz and Barcelona. She worked for Erich Prödl Associates, Walter Angonese Architekt, ARTEC Architekten and the Free University of Bozen Bolzano, Faculty of Design and Art. Currently she lives in Vienna where she works as university assistant at the Institut für Architektur und Entwerfen, Abteilung für Gebäudelehre und Entwerfen, Technische Universität Wien.

IMAGE CREDITS

T top; B bottom

The space of the exhibition as a field of action

Giovanna Borasi

p. 30, 35, 36 (B), 38 © CCA Montréal
p. 36 (T) © Maritime History Archive, Memorial University of Newfoundland
p. 40-41, 43, 45, 46-47, 48 © CCA Montréal

Anne Holtrop

p. 51, 52, 53, 56, 57, 58, 60, 61 © Anne Holtrop
p. 62-63, 64, 65 © Bas Princen
p. 67 © Anne Holtrop
p. 68-69, 70, 72 © Bas Princen

Wilfried Kuehn

p. 78, 79, 81 © Kuehn Malvezzi
p. 82-83, 84 © Giovanna Silva
p. 86 (T-B), 88 © Armin Linke

7 Rooms, 21 Perspectives

p. 91, 92, 93, 94, 95, 96, 99, 100 © Bas Princen
p. 110, 111, 112 © OFFICE Kersten Geers David Van Severen
p. 113 © Bas Princen
p. 114 © Sven Laurent

On the side of the public

Emanuela De Cecco

p. 125 (T-B), © Emanuela De Cecco
p. 128 © Wilfried Petzi

Something Fantastic

p. 137 (T-B), 140, 142, 143, 144, 145, 146-147, 148, 149, 150
© Something Fantastic

Ilka & Andreas Ruby

p. 156 © Hisao Suzuki
p 159, 161, 162-163, 165 © Ilka & Andreas Ruby

Behind the Green Door

p. 177 © ROTOR
p. 178 © OAT-ROTOR
p. 179 © ROTOR
p. 180 © Guri Idsø Viken
p. 181, 182 © ROTOR
p. 193 © Philippe De Gobert
p. 194 (T-B) © Eric Mairiaux

AKNOWLEDGMENTS

Thank you to all the contributors whose texts are contained in this book and to all those who participated in the discussions held during the preparation of this volume.

Thank you to the discussants invited to take part in the conference Displayed Spaces in March 2013: Maddalena Dalla Mura, Nina Kolowratnik and Giaime Meloni.

In particular I consider myself very fortunate for two reasons: to have received the continuous support of Eva Mair during the different phases of this work and to have had the chance to work with Jonathan Pierini, a great designer with whom I could engage in fruitful dialogue while preparing the graphic layout of the book.

Editor
Roberto Gigliotti

Editorial Assistance
Eva Mair

Text editing
Jennifer Knaeble

Proofreading
Jennifer Knaeble

Design
Jonathan Pierini

Typefaces
Portrait, Europa

Printed by:
DZA Druckerei zu Altenburg GmbH

Paper
Munken Polar, Rembrandt / R4 Cedro Granuliert

Published by:
Spector Books, Leipzig
spectorbooks.com

ISBN: 978-3-944669-69-4

Distribution in Germany, Austria and France: GVA Gemeinsame Verlagsauslieferung Göttingen GmbH & Co. KG, www.gva-verlage.de

Distribution in Switzerland: AVA Verlagsauslieferung AG, www.ava.ch

Distribution in the UK and Japan: Anagram Books Ltd www.anagrambooks.com

Distribution in the US: RAM Publications + Distribution Inc. www.rampub.com

Printed in Germany.

Cover design
Jonathan Pierini
Sabrina Vegetti

Published with support from the Free University of Bozen Bolzano